D0645540

The FrogBuster

A Girl's Guide for Survival
in the Dating Swamp

Klayne I. Rasmussen, Ph.D.
Kip S. Rasmussen, Ph.D.
Verena B. Rasmussen

Published By *IntraLife Systems Publishing*

Illustrations by Guy Francis, Provo, Utah.

Second printing: October 2002.
Third printing: December 2002

ISBN 0-9703102-0-X
Library of Congress Control Number: 2002110732

ACKNOWLEDGMENTS

Special thanks to Mary Gaddie and Libby Hyland for their help in book layout and design. Mary believed in our project. Thank you Mary. Thanks to Amy Albo for pointing us in the right direction.

Thanks to all who reviewed early manuscripts, for their helpful comments and direction. Special thanks to Becca Ballif, Tori Ballif, Claire Swenson, Amy Stephens, Carrie Carroll and Janita Anderson for all the extra effort and valuable feedback. Thanks to Ed Eynon for his support.

Special thanks to Guy Francis for his wonderful illustrations. Thanks to his wife Lorien as well.

Thanks to the Lord for his inspiration on this book and subject matter.

FOREWORD

This book is the beginning of a wonderful life-long process of discovering you. Notice we said, "life-long." The concepts and tools introduced can help you throughout your life as you continue on your journey. Many adults are still on this pursuit, but reading the FrogBuster and incorporating the ideas will put you well on the way to finding yourself. You will also increase your potential of finding a wonderful companion with whom to share your life.

It should be pointed out up-front that the intent of this book is not to "bash" boys. There are many wonderful boys in this world, just as there are many wonderful girls who have the potential of entering into very fulfilling relationships. The opposite is also true. There are both boys and girls who have relationship warts. One of the intents of this book is to help you expose the warts before you get too far into the relationship.

We believe that the marriage relationship is the most important relationship that we have in our lives and in society. It is the marital relationship that is central to the family, central to the stability of society, and central to human growth and progress. When marriages are strong, typically, families are strong. When families are strong, communities are strong. When communities are strong the nation is strengthened.

In Chapter 1 you will be introduced to Princess Kate. Princess Kate grew up in medieval times when most marriages were arranged. Her parents, being progressive as they were, decided to let Princess Kate find her own mate. To help her on her journey, a spell was cast on the kingdom, and all of the boys were turned into frogs. Princess Kate was on a quest to find her prince charming amongst the frogs, but since it was hard to distinguish the frogs from one another by their looks, she had to get to know them first. Find out where her quest leads her in this fast reading story.

In Chapters 2 and 3 you will read about different aspects of self-discovery. In Chapters 4-7 you enter the dating swamp with all the ups and downs of the murky, unsure waters. You are guided through the various stages of dating, what to expect and what not to expect. You will also be briefly introduced to important concepts in engagement and marriage so that you can be aware of them early on in your life.

Chapter 8 introduces you to the kingdom predators. Meeting up with these types of boys could happen anywhere in the process of dating and engagement. Hopefully, with the help of this book, you will be able to discover a predator before you are actually married to one. You've probably heard some men labeled as "manipulators," "chauvinists," etc., we have put new labels on these predator type men according to characteristics of predators in the animal kingdom. See if you recognize any men you know in this chapter.

TABLE OF CONTENTS

CHAPTER 1

PRINCESS KATE AND THE FROG PRINCE STORY

nce upon a time in a kingdom far away, there lived a king, a queen and their daughter, the Princess Kathryn—Kate for short. Ever since Kate was a young girl, she knew that one day a knight in shining armor would ride up and sweep her off her feet. Together, they would ride into the golden sunset and live happily ever after.

At 17, Kate had become a beautiful young woman. She was the perfect princess, quick with a smile, and always laughing and joking. Kate was friendly with all of the girls in the kingdom. They looked up to Kate, partly because she was the princess, but also because she was so easy to like.

You would think that with all these things going for her, Kate would be a self-confident person. But, like most teenage girls, she had many insecurities. She didn't think that she was all that pretty. She always thought she looked fat. Every time she started to get even the smallest pimple on her face, she was distraught, certain that everyone would see only the pimple. When she got more than one at the same time, it was as if her world turned inside out. She didn't even want to leave her room, she felt so hideous.

ier body had gone through so many confusing changes. Some she liked, it others were not so great. Her best friend, Mary, lived in a castle not far om hers, and they talked about everything: the way their bodies had hanged, the strange ways they felt, the up and down moods they went through. One minute they would be happy and the next depressed without any reasonable explanation. It was all so confusing.

It seemed that the world had become a lot more confusing too. Kate thought she knew who she was but after she was about 15 or 16 years old, everything seemed to make a little less sense. She worried more about how she looked and what clothes she wore, and at times felt unattractive. She started to notice the world and how unfair it seemed, especially her parents. In fact, she could remember when she didn't think her parents could do anything wrong, but now they seemed to be completely out of touch with reality. She remembered when she used to play all of the time without a care in the world. She longed for those carefree days.

What was particularly confusing was the whole "boy" thing. When Kate was in grade school, boys were just pests and a little creepy. But during the past few years, Kate had begun thinking that some guys were actually cute. She would get these funny feelings inside whenever she saw a good-looking guy, especially if he noticed her too. She liked the feelings but didn't know what to make of them.

She loved to get together with her girlfriends and spend hours talking about boys, and who liked who. Kate, like all her girlfriends, just wanted to have fun. And fun to them was now spelled B-O-Y-S.

Many boys tried to get Kate's attention. Each one had something that made him attractive. Kate loved the way Edward looked in his armor. She loved the way Donovan's long blonde hair would trail behind him as he rode away from the castle on his horse. She especially liked when the boys flirted with her. They would wink at her from across the room, joke with her and single her out in a crowd. Kate realized she liked boys a lot. "There are so many boys and so little time," Kate thought.

It was that broad thinking that became a bit of a problem. Kate was very particular about her clothes, her room, and her friends. However, when it came to dating, she was not very particular at all. She would date almost anyone...as long as they were good looking, or had nice armor, or dressed well. They all competed for her attention by driving the nicest chariots and competing in the kingdom jousting contests. Kate fell for it too, almost always dating the winner of the jousts or the Big Man of the Kingdom, the B-M-O-K, as the girls liked to call the hottest boy of the moment.

For a while, Kate thought Jonathon was the bomb. He had the body, the chariot, and the deepest blue eyes. When he looked at her in that certain way she just melted. When he asked her out the first time she thought she had died and gone to heaven. Dating him was like heaven...for a while. But then, he stopped calling as often. On weekend nights he would not ask her out in advance; he would just show up expecting her to be waiting for him. (Unfortunately, she would be.) He started telling her that she would look better if she wore her hair and make-up differently. He also flirted with her friends. One time she saw Jonathon and one of her "friends" sitting together in what looked like more than just a friendly situation. When she confronted him about it, he told her that they were just friends and that she was jealous. He also told her to quit spying on him and acting like she owned him.

 ate hated being treated like this but she kept dating Jonathon because, oh!, those eyes.... And besides, her girlfriends were insanely jealous of her dating such an incredible guy. When Kate told them that she was thinking of breaking up with him, they thought she was crazy. That was enough to make her rethink wanting to break up. One day, Kate found Jonathon "leaning" close to another girl while she smiled and laughed her flirtatious laugh. Kate had really had enough of Jonathon and told him that if he didn't stop flirting with other girls and change how he treated her they were through. Jonathon yelled at her and told her she was not "all that" and told her in no uncertain terms that he never wanted to see her again. So this was the "Big Breakup" she and her friends had talked so much about and had seen other girls go through but swore she would never experience. She couldn't believe that she had actually broken up with Jonathon. She certainly wasn't prepared for how she felt afterwards.

At first, Kate was very sad, even depressed. She didn't feel like eating or sleeping. She didn't feel like doing schoolwork. She certainly didn't feel much like a princess. The only thing that seemed to help her was talking to her friend Mary. It took quite a while before she felt like going out with other people again. It still hurt when she saw Jonathon, especially when he was with another girl. But once she got out and started doing things with Mary and her friends again, she felt quite a bit better. There were other guys who started to pay attention to her, and she realized that Jonathon wasn't the only game in town after all.

As it turns out, Jonathon's behavior was pretty typical of some of the BMOK's Kate dated. In the beginning, they treated Kate like the princess that she was. However, she noticed that after only a few dates the boys would start treating her poorly. You would think that Kate, being the princess and beautiful girl that she was, would have been a bit less vulnerable to being treated this way. Unfortunately, the more she dated, the more confused she became. The more confused she became, the more she dated guys that treated her poorly.

he King and Queen were concerned about Princess Kate. They were quite progressive for their times: While almost all marriages in the kingdom were arranged and had been so for ages, they had agreed from the time that Kate was in the cradle to allow her to pick her prince. The King and Queen had always trusted Princess Kate and were confident that she would pick someone who was not only worthy of their daughter, but also worthy to be a prince. As they watched the boys in the kingdom make their way in and out of their castle, they weren't impressed with any of them. They were afraid that if Princess Kate didn't start dating better guys they may have no choice but to arrange a marriage when the time came. But, they knew she may never forgive them for that.

After many months of worrying, the King and Queen decided to consult the Royal Wizard for advice. They figured if anyone could come up with something to help Kate, the Wizard could. After all, the Wizard not only knew all the tricks in the book (he'd written most of the book), he was also very wise and caring.

The Wizard welcomed the chance to speak with the King and Queen. As they told him of their concerns he agreed completely. Indeed, he had been watching all of this happen and shared their concerns. Unwise dating habits among teenagers were common enough in the kingdom, but things did seem to be especially bad lately. His biggest concern was that the situation now involved the beloved Princess. The King and Queen asked him if he had any ideas about what could be done. He told them he would need to give this situation some deep thought. He retired to his contemplation chamber and went into his thinking trance. This approach usually worked for him, and sure enough, after some serious contemplation, he formulated an amazing plan. Even he was surprised that he could be this clever.

He met with the King and Queen and explained his idea. As the Wizard's plan was laid out before them the King and Queen shifted nervously in their thrones, not anticipating such an elaborate and drastic approach. But after some discussion, the King and Queen decided they liked the idea, so the Wizard went to work concocting a spell.

This was going to be no ordinary spell. He knew it would take all his special powers. So mustering all his wizardry, he whispered and he shouted. He bounced and shook, and did everything short of turning himself inside out. He loved a good spell and this was going to be his best yet. Day and night he worked until he had the spell just the way he wanted it. Early in the morning, he stepped to the window, and feeling a bit giddy, cast the spell upon the kingdom. The exhausted Wizard (a spell like this wears out even the best of wizards), turned from the window with a wry smile and sat down to wait. He leaned back against a soft down-filled pillow and fell fast asleep.

The Wizard slept through the day and night. A new day was breaking when he was shaken awake by the King's messenger. The messenger exclaimed excitedly for him to come quickly to the window. The Wizard, not yet completely awake, stumbled to the window. He leaned heavily upon the window sill and peered out in the early light. As the day came into focus he could see large green frogs hopping around the streets. People were running every which way talking and pointing and wondering what had happened. He had done it! The boys in the kingdom had been transformed into the most beautiful (or hideous, depending on your point of view) frogs he had ever seen. He was so tickled with himself that he whirled around and danced a little jig. The messenger then handed him a note from the King and Queen expressing how pleased they were with the spell and congratulating the Wizard on his prowess.

Meanwhile, back at the castle, Princess Kate had just started out on her morning stroll to visit Mary with some great news about the wonderful date she had had the night before with her newest love interest, Max. When she left the castle she was aglow with feelings of love. But as soon as she got outside the castle grounds, her glow quickly changed to a look of horror. There were monstrously large frogs hopping all over the streets. One smiling frog hopped up to her and tried to kiss her. She shrieked in disgust and the frog leaped back in surprise.

"What are you doing? What's wrong with you?" she yelled at the stunned frog.

"What do you mean what's wrong with me? What's wrong with you? It's me, Max," exclaimed the frog.

"Right," Princess Kate replied. "And I'm a unicorn."

"What about last night down at the lake?" exclaimed Max.

Now the Princess was very confused, she knew no one else had been at the lake and she certainly had not told a soul. Clearly upset but gathering her composure, she asked "So why do you look like a frog today?"

"What are you talking about?" asked Max. He was very irritated and thought she was trying to insult him. "Well, if that's what you think, then you can kiss a fish. You never did know a good kiss when you had one," he said, doing his best to insult her back.

The Princess was indeed offended and told him that she never wanted to see him again. Max called her a few choice names and leaped off as angrily as a frog could.

The Princess was very annoyed. She looked around and saw all kinds of frogs hopping around the streets. Everyone was confused. They were watching the frogs and whispering, laughing, pointing, staring, and crying. Kate began to get an idea about who might be behind this. She got very angry and stormed back to the castle. She was going to get to the bottom of this if it was the last thing she did. Somebody was messing with her life and she was going to find out who and why.

By the time she got back to the castle and stormed into the King's court she was really upset. She threw open the door to the court, stomped inside and yelled, "What have you done with Max?"

Expecting a reaction like this but still taken back a bit, the King calmly replied "Now Kate, come and sit down so we can talk about this."

"Talk? I don't even want to look at you. What have you done with Max?" she said furiously. "He looks and hops just like a big green frog. He's slimy, wet and has the most hideous tongue I have ever seen."

"Now my dear, please come and let us explain," said the Queen.

The Princess would have none of it.

"You've cast some kind of evil spell on him haven't you! You've turned him into a frog!" she yelled. At that she turned, and mumbling something unintelligible, ran out the door and out of the castle. She had to find Mary and tell her what had happened.

She headed straight to Mary's castle. She didn't bother knocking or waiting to be let in. She knew where she was going and went straight to Mary's room. When Kate entered Mary's room she found Mary lying on her bed, face down sobbing into her pillow. Mary looked up when Kate entered the room and bawled, "What's happened to Ferdinand? What have they done to my Ferdi?"

ate was really angry now. They had done it to Mary as well. Kate told Mary that her Mother and Father and the Wizard, whom she described with a few unrepeatable words, had cast some spell on their boyfriends. Princess Kate ranted on about how her parents didn't care a bit about her feelings. If they did, she reasoned, they would never have turned Max and Ferdi into those hideous green amphibious creatures and ruined all her fun. The two of them vowed to never speak with their parents again. They spent the rest of the morning hanging out in Mary's room.

Later that afternoon, the two ventured out into the kingdom to see the extent of this evil spell. Much to their dismay, they discovered that, in fact, there wasn't one single boy walking around the kingdom, only a bunch of slimy frogs. She realized that not only had they turned Max into a frog but they had done it to all the boys in the kingdom. They then got very depressed thinking they would never date again.

Eventually, Kate did return home but avoided her parents like the plague (Never mind which plague. They all need to be avoided). For several days, she never left her bedroom, insisting that the servants bring her meals there. When the Queen put a stop to that, she arranged to eat at different times than her parents.

inally, after about six days of this, the King and Queen sent a servant to retrieve her from her room and bring her before them in the drawing room. Princess Kate was not happy being commanded to have an audience with her parents. She just thought it was another power play meant to humiliate her, so she refused to even look at the King and Queen.

The King spoke first.

"Katydid," (which was his affectionate nickname for her) "I know you are upset about this boys-being-turned-into-frogs thing. But if you will let your mother and me explain, we think that some day you will understand and know we've done this for your good."

Kate was beside herself but kept quiet because she had made the vow with Mary not to speak to her parents. This created a difficult situation because she wanted to yell at them and tell them how much she hated them right now, but she was determined not to speak, so she was forced to listen.

The Queen spoke next. "Katie, dear, I know this seems like an extreme thing the Wizard did. But we had him do it because we love you. Now that may seem just the opposite to you. You know that we want only the best for you. We've always told you we would like you to choose your own husband when the time comes. This is important to us and you have said it is important to you too. Being able to choose your own spouse is a very wonderful thing but it comes with a huge responsibility."

At this, the King chimed in, "And any responsibility of this nature can turn into a nightmare if you are not prepared for it, or if you do not take it seriously."

"Blah, blah, blah, how can I possibly take a slimy frog seriously," thought Kate, trying hard not to listen.

The Queen continued. "We've raised you to think for yourself and use good judgement and we thought you could be trusted to make good decisions. For the most part this has been the case. We decided to let you experience each of the boys you dated and learn from the relationships, even when we thought the boys were not very good influences on you. As you are maturing and getting closer to the time when you will pick a partner to marry, the stakes have become higher. Lately, it seems you've been dating boys that haven't been exactly the best for you."

"How would you know what's best for me? You think frogs are best for me!" she thought with disdain.

"You know it is very true that you'll eventually marry someone you date," the Queen added. "We want you to marry someone who is a positive influence, someone who encourages you to be the beautiful person that you are, someone that cherishes you and allows you to grow and become the woman you have the potential to be."

Kate was still trying not to listen, but this last bit actually made some sense to her. She too had noticed some of the guys she had dated made her feel less like a princess and more like a servant. Still, she was not about to discuss this with her "evil" parents.

"A case in point is Max. Since you've been dating him," explained the King, "you have become distant from us. You seldom speak with us. You don't tell us what you are doing or where you are going or how long you will be. You changed your hair. You changed the style of clothes you wear. You changed your make-up. You haven't been spending as much time with your friends, like Mary. Your grades are down. And you never ride your horse anymore. These are only a few of the changes we've noticed."

Kate was still angry, but her parents were making sense, too much for her liking. She had truly missed spending time riding her beloved horse. She also missed spending time with Mary and her other friends. But she had rationalized that it was because she was so in love with Max that she wanted to spend all her time with him. She wanted to do everything to make him happy so that he would love her as much as she loved him. "How could it be so wrong to do that for someone you love?" she thought.

The Queen explained further. "We were so concerned that we consulted the Wizard for some advice. You know, Katie dear, how highly he thinks of you. The Wizard noticed that you were always dating the boys who were the best-looking or who drove the fanciest chariots, basing your decisions about who to date solely on appearances. So the Wizard created a spell to level the playing field. If all the single men looked the same, that is like frogs, you would have to learn to see past the external looks and really get to know each of them before deciding if you wanted to be with them."

"Do not despair, my Katydid," said the King. "We are confident that you will find your true Prince Charming. It's just that you've gotten off track lately and we wanted to do what we could to help."

"Part of the Wizard's plan is that the frogs will not realize they are frogs. They will see themselves and each other just as they had before. That way, they will not alter their behavior, but will continue to act just as they had before the spell was cast," the Queen elaborated. "When you are certain that you are truly in love and feel that the timing is right, a simple kiss will turn him back into a young man and the spell will be broken. If, however, he is not the right man for you," the Queen continued a little sheepishly, "he will remain a frog."

The Princess was dumbstruck. Not only had they taken away her precious Max, but now they informed her that she would only be able to date frogs. And if she were ever to have another kiss it would have to be with a frog. She was too stunned to even be angry. She definitely needed some time to think this over and so she broke her own vow of silence and asked in an almost breathless tone if she could be excused.

It took a while for Kate to get back to her room. She was so confused. She felt like running away. She felt like hiding in her room for the rest of her life. But most of all, she felt like crying, and that is what she did.

It took her all the next month to get used to seeing only girls and frogs at school. All the frogboys carried on as they usually did, but she and the girls started to notice a certain "croakiness" in the boys' voices when they spoke to the girls in a rude or mean way. It was a very annoying sound and it seemed that some of the frogs' voices were always croaky, especially, and most unfortunately, Max's. Other frogs, seldom if ever sounded croaky. Kate found herself laughing and enjoying herself when she was talking to them. The other girls noticed the same thing.

Max, and many other BMOKs, couldn't figure out why the girls weren't interested in talking to them. Even more maddening to them, was why some of the dweebs were getting so much attention. So, in typical male fashion, they tried to prove their superiority by picking fights. The problem was their forearms were now too short to allow them to throw a good punch or even wrap a guy up in a headlock. They were reduced to hopping about and flicking their tongues out at each other. It was humiliating. They looked in the mirror and saw the same studly guy that they knew and loved, but the world around them was definitely a changin'.

ll the single girls in the Kingdom started to feel comfortable talking and even flirting a bit with the amphibians. They also noticed that they were getting back to being their old selves again. Kate realized she didn't really like the way she had been wearing her hair (she liked it long and flowing and Max had always wanted it curled a certain way). She started to take long rides on her horse and she was playing the harp again. She realized these two activities had carried her through many trying times, allowing her time to think and get away. Now they helped her even more.

Life generally improved and Kate was happier every day. But there was still one thing that worried her: How would she ever discover her prince so the spell would be broken? She wasn't just thinking of herself, but she felt an enormous responsibility toward all the girls in the kingdom. Kate felt that it was her duty to represent their feelings to the King and Queen. She was clearly still upset with them, but by now they were on limited speaking terms. So one night at dinner she explained that the girls in the kingdom were worried that the spell would never be broken.

The King and Queen could see that the Princess was very concerned. Truthfully, they had really only been thinking of their precious Kate, not all the other girls in the kingdom. They knew they had to do something, so they called on the Wizard to teach Kate and the girls in the kingdom about what to look for in guys and relationships.

The idea of learning about herself and relationships from someone like the Wizard was intriguing to Kate. In fact, she felt herself becoming rather enthusiastic about the idea. This was the first time in many weeks that Kate had shown any real sign of enthusiasm. It surprised her parents as well, and they were thrilled to see a spark of the old Katydid they knew and loved. Both the King and the Queen privately shouted for joy. Maybe they had made the right choice after all!

Kate and the girls in the kingdom started dating guys who treated them nicely and with respect. They started dating guys who liked them for who they were, not who they wanted them to become. Interestingly, the girls started finding it easier to accept the guys for who they were rather than always wishing that they would change this trait or that trait in order to be "perfect."

"No one is perfect," the Wizard would say, "the key is to figure out which traits are acceptable and which are not."

A curious thing happened as a result of all this: the girls in the kingdom started having a lot more fun. Kate started dating guys who shared her interests: good music, horses, laughter, and being nice to other people. And because she, and the other girls, were having such a great time dating, she sort of forgot about finding her "one and only Prince Charming." The pressure was off. It was just fun getting to know different guys.

Eventually, after a few more years of fun dating, she did meet an awesome frogboy named Daniel. He seemed to have all the important traits she wanted in a guy. He adored Princess Kate and wanted to spend his life with her. She fell in love with him. Daniel discovered over time that all the boys in the kingdom looked like frogs and that it would take a kiss from the Princess with her true Prince to break the spell. Because he loved her so much, he hoped he would be the one to break the spell. His love for Kate continued to grow and when the day for the "big kiss" came he and Kate were both very nervous.

After a quiet dinner together they went on a walk along their favorite lakeshore like they had done numerous times before. The moon was full and the reflection shimmered softly on the water. The Spring air was perfect, not too cool nor too hot, but they both were sweating a bit from nerves. They talked very little as they walked along holding hands. Stopping in their favorite place, an old oak tree stump where they had spent many evenings talking and enjoying each other's company, Daniel turned to Kate and hesitating only briefly leaned over and kissed her gently on the lips. Kate, closed her eyes, afraid of what might not happen.

Kate had wondered many times what it would be like to actually kiss a cold slimy frog. She noticed, however, that as Daniel's lips met hers they were not cold or slimy at all but warm and gentle. She never thought it would feel so good to be kissed. She never wanted it to end.

When they stopped the kiss, Daniel spoke her name softly. She could feel the love in his voice but she was still afraid to open her eyes. After what seemed like an eternity she slowly opened one eye then the other. What she saw took her breath away. Before her stood the most handsome man she had ever seen. Daniel was big and strong and his eyes were deep and warm, filled with love towards her. Her heart leaped. Standing before her was truly her Prince Charming. She knew it because she already knew what kind of man Daniel was. She would have loved him no matter what he looked like. But she was even more pleased that he was as handsome as his personality.

Kate leaped up, and throwing her arms around his neck cried, "It worked, it worked, it worked. You're a man. You're a prince. You are my Prince Charming!" At this Daniel let go a yell of joy, threw his arms around Kate, and lifting her off the ground, the two of them twirled round and round kissing and hugging and crying and laughing all at the same time. They had found each other. The spell had finally been broken.

After expressing their love for each other they couldn't wait to get back to the castle to tell the King and Queen. They hurried as fast as they could. Running into the throne room they found the King, Queen and the Wizard all waiting anxiously for them to return. Kate and Daniel didn't need to say a word. The King, Queen and Wizard could see that Daniel had been transformed into a man by the kiss of the Princess. They knew that he was not only a prince but that he would be a great king. Daniel, a true gentleman, formally asked the King for his daughter's hand in marriage. The King gladly consented and plans for the grandest wedding of all time were set into motion.

he following year, Kate and Daniel were married, and it was a happy day indeed. As soon as they said, "I do," the frog spell was broken throughout the entire kingdom. Most of the boys returned to their boyish selves again. The girls were ecstatic, but they had learned their lessons. They knew what to look for in a guy and what to avoid. The guys too had learned some lessons along the way. They had learned to treat the girls with respect and honor.

*And as for Kate and Daniel... Of course they lived happily ever after.
No good fairy tale would end otherwise.*

**Reality note: They did have a few conflicts along the way, but worked
through them and remained happily ever after.*

Chapter 2

PRELUDE TO THE KISS: DISCOVERING YOU

his chapter is all about you. That's right, YOU! Let's just leave the boys out of it for a minute (or at least until Chapter 4) and figure out who you are and what you want out of life. As you've probably already realized, this is not an easy task, in fact, it may be a lifelong pursuit.

YOUNG AND RESTLESS

f you're a typical teenager, you probably feel like you're walking around in a sort of cloudy haze wondering who you are and how you fit into this crazy world. Your body is changing, your hormones have kicked into gear, your face is breaking out, and you care a lot about what everyone else thinks of you. Rest assured, you're not alone. It's a rare teenager who hasn't been kept awake at night wondering, "Who am I?" "How do I fit in?" "Am I normal?" "Does anybody else feel like this?" You're going through a confusing period of development and change.

You've probably noticed that your body is changing. You may still be waiting for some parts to come in. Or you may have already received an early shipment. You may have noticed that your hips are getting a little wider, your breasts are starting to change and your waist may be getting smaller in relation to your hips and shoulders. Your face may be getting thinner, wider or just generally changing shape. The hair on your head may even be changing, getting thicker or changing color. You're probably getting hair other places where it hasn't been noticeable before such as on your legs, under your arms, and in the pubic area. You may have started your menstrual cycle with its accompanying side effects (body cramps, irritability, and headaches) that many girls experience. You may have noticed that you're more emotional, sometimes getting weepy or upset by the smallest things, like your sister borrowing a shirt without asking, or a pimple blossoming on your face, or your parents commenting on the type of clothes you are wearing. You might remember when things like this had very little effect on you, but now they seem huge.

Hormones (body chemicals) that are being released by your body bring on all these changes. Hormones make your body change in preparation for adulthood, and for becoming a mother. The changes in your body are all part of a process that usually begins when you become a teenager. Some girls start to see these changes as early as 10 years old and some girls don't see them until they are 16 or 17. But all girls go through it. It's normal. It's expected. It's part of becoming a woman. These changes are called "puberty."

Puberty is a confusing time for most girls, and is usually very hard to talk about, especially to adults. Teenage girls can cry and laugh within minutes -

both at the same subject, feeling loving and enraged, close and distant - all at the same time. One minute they're up, the next they're down. These feelings are all jumbled and need to be sorted out somehow. Teenage girls are also faced with mixed messages from the outside world. Be smart, but not too smart. Be pretty, but beauty isn't everything. Be thin, but stay healthy. Be popular, but not a snob. Achieve, but don't be threatening. Be sexy, but not a sex object.

If you're in your 20's, you're probably thinking, "Ahh, if I only knew then what I know now." You might even be nostalgic for those teenage years, when life seemed relatively carefree. But then again, maybe not. Now you probably feel saddled with more serious life challenges such as school, career, and relationship decisions.

Your body and mind are still changing. You've probably become accustomed to your body and the shape it has taken on. Your body should be settling into a fairly consistent routine. For instance, your periods should be pretty regular and typically your mood swings mellow out a bit in your 2Os. If they aren't, you should get a checkup with your doctor and tell him or her about what's going on with your body.

You've probably been dating for quite a while, had a few steady boyfriends or many different dates. If so, you have undoubtedly dated a few frogs and maybe even worse critters. You may have also dated a few princes, whether you knew it or not.

Your brain is also different than it was a few years ago. You think differently, many times in a more logical way because of things you've learned and experiences you have had. Hopefully, minor things in your life (like the pimple on your face) can be kept in perspective as minor now, instead of the major catastrophe it once was when you were a teenager.

Life in general probably still seems a bit confusing and also a little heavier. You're getting more serious about life and also about dating. Now, with guys you start to get close to you may be thinking, "This could be the guy I marry." You may even have had a boyfriend by now that you have thought about marrying.

These changes are all part of becoming an adult. They can be scary and they can be exciting. Again, everybody goes through these changes. They are normal.

GETTING TO KNOW YOU

hether you are a teenager or young adult, before you start making big life decisions it's important that you get to know yourself and what you want out of life. Once you have a good understanding of who you are, lots of things in life will become clearer, including what you're looking for in a guy.

So, before you start kissing a lot of frogs to see if one could be a prince for you, let's first figure out YOU.

WHO YOU ARE AND WHAT YOU ARE TRYING TO FIND?

This book is about the dating process (some might call it the dating game) and how to get the most out of it by avoiding the frogs. But discovering YOU and liking what you find, or changing so that you do like YOU, is even more important than the dating process.

Hopefully, this book will help you discover some tools for happiness in your life. After all, happiness is what most of us want from life. An important thing to remember is that happiness is not a destination; it is a "state of being" while on your journey.

Some people, both girls and guys alike, are mistaken in the notion that if they could just obtain a certain thing in life, then they would be happy. Kellie was always looking for that something else in life to make her happy. When she was in junior high, she just knew that as soon as she started high school she would be happy. She started high school and wasn't happy.

She knew that as soon as she had a boyfriend, then she would be happy. She got a boyfriend, but wasn't happy.

She knew that as soon as she graduated from high school she would be happy. She graduated from high school. She still wasn't happy.

She knew that when she started college and moved away from home she would be happy. She started college and moved away from home and guess what, she still wasn't happy.

When she graduated from college she thought she would be happy. She graduated and wasn't happy.

When she got married she thought she would be happy. She got married and wasn't happy.

When they could afford to buy a house, she would be happy. They bought a house and she wasn't happy.

When they had their first child she would be happy. They had their first child and she still wasn't happy.

This story may seem silly and unrealistic. The sad thing about it is that this story has happened over and over. The point of Kellie's story is you need to find happiness at whatever stage you are at in life. If you are not generally happy, acquiring things or different stages in life will not change your outlook. Learn to be happy if you are a teenager, adult, single, married, separated, divorced, widowed, poor, rich, healthy, sickly, or whatever your situation. You will also learn that other people like to be around happy people! You may have heard the phrase, "Misery loves company." Happiness loves company, too. If you want happy people around you, you need to be happy yourself and with yourself.

An important part of happiness is understanding who you are, what you expect, and how you perceive your world—once you can answer these questions you are on your way to becoming a complete person.

BECOMING A COMPLETE PERSON

An important key to completeness is learning how to value yourself. This is true no matter what you look like, where you live, what your talents are, or who your family is. Accepting yourself with all your imperfections is the foundation of becoming a complete person.

None of us are perfect, and very few of us think we are. The problem is that sometimes we think others are. Then we think we are inferior or not as good. We get the mistaken idea that if we could just change our hair or our height or if we just had a smaller butt or bigger breasts, or if we just weighed less we would be accepted by others—and then we would be happy. Well, the reality is, while you may think these changes would make everything all right, they don't. If you are looking for that 'one more thing' or the 'one more change' to make you happy, you will be chasing happiness your entire life.

Sharon was not so different from Princess Kate. She was one of the most popular girls in high school. She was a cheerleader from her sophomore year all through her senior year. She was good looking. She was smart and got good grades. She dated the best looking guys—many of whom were older. Her family had plenty of money. They lived in a very nice house, and she always drove a nice car. She seemed to have it all. But not long after completing high school she got pregnant, had an abortion, and was almost disowned by her family. Fifteen years later, at her high school reunion Sharon was talking with a classmate who was a marriage therapist and made the comment, "You should do a group session with all the cheerleaders. We all have terrible marriages." She was very unhappy with her life and marriage. She had had at least one affair. She still had plenty of money and lived a very "comfortable" lifestyle. She had always looked for her sense of acceptance and happiness through what she had, who she dated, what type of profession she or her husband did, and what she looked like. According to what she believed, having all these things (marriage, nice house, money, kids, popularity) should have brought her happiness. But even in her 30's she was unhappy. She was very dissatisfied with her life and was still looking for answers. She had been looking in all the wrong places. She had been searching all her life for happiness outside of herself.

Real happiness and a sense of completeness comes from being the best person you can be. It comes from accepting yourself for who you are, living well and helping others do the same. Living well means being good to yourself and to others. It means taking care of yourself. It means standing up for what is right and for your rights as a person. It comes from knowing where you are going and why you are going there.

If you are not happy with your life, if you feel a void or emptiness, it's safe to say that you are not happy with YOU. If this sounds like you, then dating, relationships, and especially marriage, will not make your life any better. In fact, many times dating and marriage make it worse, especially if you have not achieved peace and contentment within yourself. This doesn't mean you should avoid relationships and marriage if you don't feel complete, it means continue to work on yourself and you'll have better relationships overall.

The place to start "looking for love" is within you. The healthiest perspective to take on life and with which to enter any dating relationship is: "I'm OK alone." This may sound odd in a book about being with others, but after a little explanation it should make more sense. When you feel comfortable with who you are and don't need someone else in your life to make you feel whole, then you are ready to share your life with someone. If you choose to be in a relationship because you "want" it, not because you "need" it, then it has a better chance of being satisfying.

You have probably heard some people refer to their partner as their "better half." While this is usually meant as a compliment, it implies that you and your partner are only whole together. A healthy couple should be two whole or complete persons, who know what they want and who work to accomplish their goals and dreams together. A Chinese proverb says that when two halves come together, they make a whole, but when two wholes come together, there is eternal light and beauty.

So if you don't feel like a whole person yet don't make the mistake of getting in a relationship thinking it will make your life alright. Keep in mind that it is better to stay single than to date or marry out of desperation or fear of being alone. You will be better off in a relationship if you believe that YOU are a wonderful person with or without a partner and you deserve to be happy. When you get to that point in your life you will be able to say "I'm OK alone." Once you can say that with conviction to yourself you will be in a great place emotionally to enter into a meaningful relationship, that will, in fact, bring you more satisfaction and happiness.

Being a complete person does not mean being perfect. Nobody is perfect, although many of us think we should be and spend a great amount of time and effort trying to be. It means accepting all parts of you as you are, moving on in your life, working on those things that you want to improve and being open to opportunities for growth on your journey. It also means accepting others for who they are and giving them the space they need to grow on their journey

IT'S ALL IN YOUR PERSPECTIVE

 here do you "get" happiness? Great question. The place to start is with YOU. All other aspects of your life can add depth and meaning, but you are the only one that can make you happy.

You choose whether to be happy or sad, it's all how you look at things. It's your perspective, how you interpret things and how you make sense of your life. Perspective is defined by what you pay attention to, by what you think is important, and by how you see the world and you in it. Think back on how Princess Kate thought that she wasn't very pretty but all the other girls in the kingdom thought she had it all. That is perspective! Kate was paying attention to all her faults. The rest of the girls were paying attention to her strengths. Kate also interpreted her boyfriends' negative comments as being a true reflection of her. She was choosing what she would pay attention to. She was showing her perspective.

Your perspective means that you see things differently from everybody else. Nobody else will see things or understand life's events the same way you will, even if they experience the same exact event that you do. That's because perspective also has to do with how you interpret those events you experience. And how you interpret those events determines the meaning they have for you in your life, whether good or bad, helpful or hurtful, functional or dysfunctional.

WHERE ARE YOU COMING FROM?

Take this quiz to find out more about your perspective.

1. When you see a glass of water that is filled halfway do you see the glass as half empty-or half-full?
   Half-empty ☐   Half-full ☐

2. Do you often feel defeated even before you begin a big project?
   Yes ☐   No ☐

3. Do you often see life as being unfair or as a challenge to make the most of?
   Unfair ☐   Challenge ☐

4. Do you often feel like giving up in tough situations because you feel that you are unable to change things?
   Yes ☐   No ☐

5. Do you often feel that bad events are your fault?
   Yes ☐   No ☐

6. Do you often think that bad events will last a long time?
   Yes ☐   No ☐

7. Do you often feel that a failure is a long lasting thing or do you see it as a temporary setback or challenge?
   Long Lasting ☐   Temporary setback ☐

8. Do you often feel more helpless than hopeful for the future?
   Yes ☐   No ☐

9. Do you often spend a lot of time thinking about problems?
   Yes ☐   No ☐

10. Do you often find negative when others see positive?
    Yes ☐   No ☐

In the questions how many did you pick that were the first answer, and how many did you pick that were the second answer? If you picked the first answer more than 3 times then you are likely more pessimistic and negative about your world. If you picked the first answer three or less times then you are likely more optimistic and positive about your world.

Like the first question in the quiz above, some people will look at a half-filled glass and say it is half-full. Others will look at the same glass and say it is half-empty. That is both perspective and interpretation.

Those seeing the glass as half-full are typically referred to as being optimistic, or seeing the more positive side of life. This perspective offers many advantages because it allows you to see the potential that exists for things to be good and to get better.

Those seeing the glass as half-empty are typically referred to as being pessimistic, or seeing the more negative side of life. Pessimistic people tend to interpret things in life as being more dramatic and have more of a sense of hopelessness. They tend to enjoy life less, and typically find less fulfillment out of who they are and what life is handing them

Jill and Sandra were in the same class in school. They were both equally smart and capable of getting good grades, but Jill was an 'A' student and Sandra was a 'C' student. The difference was that Jill saw class assignments as being given to stimulate her thinking and to help her learn. She didn't necessarily like to do the homework, but she knew that if she did she would learn the material and earn a good grade. She also had the goal of going to college and hoped to be able to do so on a scholarship so she worked even harder to maintain her good grades. Sandra, on the other hand, saw class assignments as a way the teacher used to punish her, to keep her from being with friends after school and causing her grief in life. She simply refused to do most of the assignments and turned in only those that she could get done in class. She had no plans for college or further schooling. She thought school was just something that she had to do because it was the law.

Jill and Sandra had pretty much the same ability to understand and do school work. One chose to see the positive in school and to succeed, the other chose to see the negative and not succeed. It's all a matter of perspective.

How you perceive the world will make a huge difference when it comes to how much you enjoy life. It also has a profound effect on how happy you are.

How you perceive such things as a break-up, being jealous of someone, feeling that life is unfair, for instance, will determine how you react and the effect it has on you.

The reason you should give your perspective some serious thought before acting on a whim is that, like Princess Kate, we often choose to pay attention to and place importance on the wrong things. For instance, we let what others say mean more to us than it should. Kate was not ugly. She was not fat. Her hair didn't need to be changed. But every time a guy that she liked told her that she would look better if she changed something, she believed him. And change she did.

Another common saying about perspective is "The grass is always greener on the other side of the fence." What this means is that no matter how good we have it, we look at someone or something else and think that it would be better if we were that person or had that something. People do this in relationships all the time.

People often look at someone else's relationship and think, "I would be so much happier if I had him for a husband/boyfriend." The reality is that when you get to the "other side of the fence" you find that it is the same old grass or sometimes you even find out the grass is moldy. Don't get caught wishing you had something else thinking it would make your life better. It won't. YOU are the someone or something that will make your life better. This is perspective.

Let's look at another example of how perspective can affect the way you experience your world.

Let's say, for instance, that you are coming home from school having just received your report card. You have been used to getting "B's" and "C's" but because of your hard work you earned all "A's". You would be feeling pretty good about yourself. As you walk in the door your little brother comes running past and tells you how stupid you are and then runs away as fast as he can. He's done this plenty of times before and usually you get upset and run after him. But today his remark is received very differently. You are feeling so good that you don't even pay the slightest attention to him. After a few seconds your brother comes back around the corner with a look on his face like "What's wrong with you?" He is so used to you chasing him after such a comment that he is completely baffled about your lack of reaction. Again, you don't care. You are feeling so good that you don't even take notice.

Pretty great, huh?

Now let's look at a little different situation. Let's say you are on your way home from school with a report card that is all "C's" and "D's" when you are used to getting "A's" and "B's". Not only that, your mom and dad have told you that if you ever get a "D" you would be grounded — no phone, no friends, no car, not a single luxury. Imagine your different mood. As you go in the door your bratty little brother comes running by and calls you stupid. How do you think you are going to react this time? You take off after him and when you catch him you teach him a lesson about brains he is never going to forget.

Pretty ugly, huh?

The difference in the two situations is how you felt. In the first situation your brother hardly bothered you at all. In the second situation you wanted to rid yourself of having a brother all together. The situations were the same except for how you felt about yourself and what you let bother you.

When you don't feel good about yourself, or when you are in a bad mood (such as when that dreaded PMS monster is looming, or you break up with a boyfriend), how easy is it to get you upset? It's probably not very hard. Even the littlest things can irritate you when you feel like that. Similarly, when you aren't feeling that you are very good or worth very much, even the slightest negative comment about you can be devastating. You will take it at face value not even considering the possibility that it may not be true. Then, just like that, you think you are a horrible, terrible, no good, very bad, worth-nothing person. This, too, is perspective. It is how you view yourself that allows the negative comment to have power.

The wife of a former president of the United States, Eleanor Roosevelt, once made a very wise statement about self-perspective. She said, "No one can make you feel inferior without your permission." What she is saying is that no one can control how you feel but you. You have the power to choose your perspective. Even if you have the bad grades you can still choose not to pay attention to your bratty little brother's annoying comments. If you choose to feel bad or accept someone's negative comments about you, that is entirely up to you. You have the power to choose, no matter what your background, no matter how good or bad your life has been, no matter where you came from: rich or poor, happy or sad. Understanding this is one of the keys to real happiness and fulfillment in life.

Perspective has a lot to do with how you experience life. How you experience life is directly connected with how satisfied and happy you are. You have complete control over your perspective. If your perspective is more on the negative side then you can change it. You can decide if you are going to see the cup as half full rather than half empty. If you are not happy then you can change that too.

Try this little experiment for just a minute. Try frowning as big a frown as you can. Hold the frown for 5-10 seconds. While you are holding the frown think about how you are feeling. Now relax your face for a few seconds. Next make a great big smile. Hold it for 5-10 seconds and while holding it notice how you feel. If you are like most people while you were frowning you felt a little negative or bad, but while you were smiling things were more positive and you felt better than when you were frowning.

This simple experiment shows you how much influence you have over how you feel. The next time you are upset or feeling hurt just try smiling and see if that simple act doesn't change things for the better, even if only in a small way. See if it doesn't change your perspective just a little. Even a little change is positive and can get you on the road to feeling better and having more happiness

YOUR PERSONALITY

he idea of perspective and how you look at the world is a big part of who you are. Your perspective is influenced greatly by your personality. Personality is a fancy way of describing the kind of person you are. Have you ever noticed how some people are so perky and others so grumpy, how some are mellow, and some are excitable, how some are serious while others are light hearted? Do any of these describe you? All of these are describing aspects of personality.

Your personality is who you are, how you act, how things affect you, the things you like and dislike, your sociability, your attitudes, your emotions, your moods. No one else in the universe has the same personality as you. You are unique. Your unique personality is one of the major things that others are attracted to or want to avoid, as the case may be.

Personality also has a lot to do with how others see you. You may have heard people say such things as, "She is so happy," or "She has a way of making others feel so good, I just love being around her." You also hear, "She is hard to get along with," or "She is so negative all of the time it just brings me down." These are statements about a person's personality.

Some personalities are more attractive to most people than others, but what you will find is that almost every personality is attractive to someone.

What you must decide is what type of personality traits you have and if you want to change any of them, or develop others. In considering changing any part of your personality you should understand that your personality is fairly well established by now. In fact, it was mostly established by the time that you were about five years old. While you may not be able to change your entire personality (we hope you don't want to), specific personality traits can be changed, although it will take a lot of effort, attention and sticking to it.

A NOISY NINE-YEAR-OLD

Jared was an outspoken, noisy nine-year-old. He loved to run and play and shout and yell. Most of his verbal communication was yelling or talking loudly. This trait disturbed most people around him. His mother and father tried to get him to lower his voice. He would try but very soon he would be back to the same old Jared. One day an uncle who Jared liked very much was visiting and noticed how loud Jared was. This uncle took Jared aside and explained to him when he was a kid about Jared's age he too had been very loud. As he got older he came to realize that people were very disturbed by his loud voice and that many of his friends stopped wanting to be around him because he was so loud. He made a decision to change his loud voice and be softer with others. Jared determined that he too would become quieter. There were many times that he forgot and would begin yelling again. But Jared didn't let the slip-ups discourage him. He just kept on working at it. It took him many years to feel that he had actually become quieter. But he did change that personality trait.

THE NEIGHBORHOOD BULLY

When Andrew was young, he was quite mean to others. In fact, one girl in his neighborhood was very afraid of him. She use to walk clear around the block to avoid passing his house. Andrew really didn't know he was that mean. It was just the way he had of surviving. Later, Andrew played football in high school and was known as one of the meanest, hardest tacklers in the league. He found that people congratulated him for being such a good hitter on the field. But Andrew also noticed that when he was mean off the field people avoided him. His girlfriends didn't stay around long either because he wasn't always very nice to them. Andrew was a smart guy and began to notice this trend. He didn't like it because he liked being with people. He decided that he was going to be nice off the field. He worked at it and worked at it. People noticed a difference but it wasn't until several years later at a high school reunion that he ran into the girl from his neighborhood. She told him that she used to be afraid of him and was amazed at the complete difference in him.

THE GALLOPING GOSSIP

Meg was a very popular girl all through school. She had lots of friends and she was involved in most school activities. The one thing about Meg that bothered most people who knew her was that she was a terrible gossip. She would talk about people behind their backs and tried to create alliances with girls. Meg was a lot like Princess Kate. In spite of her popularity, she was insecure about herself. That is why she gossiped. She was afraid that no one would like her, which, by the way, was what eventually happened. By the time she was a senior in high school, she didn't have anybody that she could call a friend. She still was involved in all the school events, but hardly any girls would hang out with her. One day she was talking to Sherri who she respected a lot. She started to gossip about another girl, trying to create an alliance with Sherri against this girl. Sherri stopped Meg. She told Meg that if Meg wanted to have friends, especially her, that Meg would have to stop gossiping about others. Sherri told Meg that she was a very likeable person and people would want to be her friend if she would just stop gossiping about everybody.

Meg took this to heart. She decided that she would stop the gossip. But she also asked Sherri if she would help her do it. Sherri agreed and supported Meg in her quest. It wasn't long before the other girls began to notice that Sherri and Meg were hanging out together. That surprised them because they all thought Sherri was cool, and didn't expect her to hang with Meg. They also noticed that Meg wasn't talking about others anymore. They were suspicious of Meg because she had been such a gossip for so long. Eventually they began accepting the new Meg. Meg noticed that she didn't have to gossip to keep friends. In fact, she found that the other girls were much nicer to her after she stopped gossiping. She realized that her insecurity had created exactly what she was afraid of happening—not having any friends. She was very grateful to Sherri for helping her change a personality trait and grow to be a better person.

Just like the people in these examples you can change something that you don't like about your personality. The other thing to consider is that you can also develop your positive traits so that you become even better at them. Traits that you like and that seem to be attractive to others such as a good sense of humor, enthusiasm for life, caring about yourself and others, being hard working, dedicated, goal oriented, well educated, wise and so forth can become even stronger. It is fairly easy to build upon your positive traits.

Eliminating a negative trait can be much more difficult, but it can be done. You might be wondering how you could identify your positive traits that you want to build upon and the negative traits you want to eliminate.

We all have positive and negative character traits, but some of them are not obvious to us. These are what we call personality "blind spots." Other people, however, can see these traits clearly. If you find that people generally have the same reaction to you, and that reaction is negative, it is important to ask yourself whether these people have identified one of your blind spots and whether aspects of your personality are turning other people off. This has to do with your perspective of the world based on what you don't see about yourself, and on the perspective of others according to what they may be seeing about you.

A good general rule is that if three people who don't know each other tell you the same thing about your personality, you should take notice. Then, if a certain trait is identified, it is important for you to ask yourself if you want to keep those parts of your personality which seem to be pushing other people away. It's always your decision as to whether you want to change.

Most of us want to be better and to have a better life. This usually means eliminating negative traits and strengthening positive ones. The following exercise can help you identify some traits that you may have or may want to develop.

Look at the list of personality traits in the following Personality Trait chart. Circle each trait you think describes you. Be sure to go through the whole list and circle as many traits as you like. The key here is to be very honest with yourself.

PERSONALITY CHART

ACTIVE	HARDWORKING	ABRASIVE	PESSIMISTIC
AGREEABLE	HEALTHY	AGGRESSIVE	PROCRASTINATES
ANALYTIC	HONEST	ANNOYING	RIGID OR INFLEXIBLE
ASSERTIVE	HOPEFUL	ARROGANT	SELF-CENTERED
CAPABLE	HUMOROUS	ARGUMENTATIVE	SELFISH
CAREFUL	IMAGINATIVE	BLAMES OTHERS	SLOTHFUL
CARING	INDEPENDENT	BOSSY	SUBMISSIVE
CHEERFUL	INSIGHTFUL	BRAGGY	UNDEPENDABLE
COMMUNICATIVE	INTELLIGENT	CLOSE MINDED	UNKIND
COMPETENT	LEADER	DEPENDENT ON OTHERS	UNEDUCATED
CONFIDENT	LIKES VARIETY	DISAGREEABLE	UNMOTIVATED
CONSCIENTIOUS	LOVING	DISHONEST	UNREALISTIC
CONSERVATIVE	METHODICAL	DISORGANIZED	UNREASONABLE
CONSIDERATE	MOTIVATED	DISRESPECTFUL	UNRELIABLE
COOPERATIVE	OPEN MINDED	EASILY ANGERED	UPTIGHT
COURAGEOUS	ORGANIZED	EASILY DISCOURAGED	WEAK
COURTEOUS	OUTGOING	EASILY DISTRACTED	WORRIED
CREATIVE	PATIENT	EASILY INFLUENCED	
CURIOUS	PERSISTENT	FEARFUL	
DETAIL ORIENTED	PRACTICAL	GIVE UP EASILY	
DEDICATED	PREPARED	GOSSIPY	
DEEP-THINKING	REALISTIC	IMPULSIVE	
DEPENDABLE	REASONABLE	IMPATIENT	
DETERMINED	RELIABLE	IMPRUDENT	
DISCIPLINED	RESPECTFUL	INSECURE	
EASY GOING	RESPONSIBLE	IRRESPONSIBLE	
ENERGETIC	SECURE	IRRITABLE	
EVEN TEMPERED	SELF-AWARE	JEALOUS	
FAIR	SELF-CONFIDENT	LAZY	
FLEXIBLE	SELF-STARTER	MEAN SPIRITED	
FOCUSED	SPIRITUAL	NARROW-MINDED	
FOLLOWER	SPONTANEOUS	NEGATIVE	
FRIENDLY	THOUGHTFUL	OVERLY PERFECTIONISTIC	
FUNNY	UNSELFISH	OVERLY SKEPTICAL	
GOAL-ORIENTED	WISE	PASSIVE	

After you have circled all the traits in the chart that you feel describe you, look at the ones you circled. Count how many you circled in the first two columns. Count how many you circled in the third and fourth columns. The traits in the first two columns are generally considered to be positive personality traits and tend to indicate that you have a more positive outlook on life and you see yourself in a more positive light. It also says that you view life as a challenge rather than a burden.

The traits in the right two columns are generally considered negative personality traits. The traits tend to indicate that you have a more negative perspective on life, you see yourself in a more negative way and you tend to blame others or outside events for things that go wrong in your life.

You should look at this exercise in two ways. One way is to count up the number of traits circled in each of the positive and negative columns. If you circled more in the positive or negative columns, then that should give you information about how you view life.

The second way to look at this is to look at the traits you circled and decide which traits you want to change in yourself, if any. For example, if you feel that life is "out to get you" and you circled traits in the negative columns such as: blames others, impatient, irresponsible or submissive, these traits give you insight into how you view yourself. These are traits you can work on if you so choose.

Now, beside each trait write what evidence you have that makes you think you have that trait. Your evidence could be anything such as "My friends or family say this about me," or "I do this when such and such happens," or "People laugh at my jokes," or "I often get compliments about this trait."

PERSONALITY TRAIT EXERCISE

Personality Trait   Evidence

_____   _____

_____   _____

_____   _____

_____   _____

_____   _____

_____   _____

If you know somebody that you trust or that knows you well, you could ask him or her if they agree with your list on Page 41. Listen to their feedback.They may not see the same traits as you do. And they may not agree with your list. Either way, this is OK. You are simply gathering information about what you see and what other people see about you. Neither your list nor the feedback you get from your trusted friends or family should be considered final and absolute.

Next, on the lines below write six personality traits that would be part of your ideal personality—whether you circled them or not. Next to the trait write what you think it would take to develop that trait.

PERSONALITY TRAIT EXERCISE

Personality Trait   How to Develop the Trait

_____   _____

_____   _____

_____   _____

_____   _____

_____   _____

_____   _____

Now look at the first and the second list. Compare them. Are there any similarities? How are they different?

The idea with personality is that you have a unique personality. No one else has the same mix of traits. No one else thinks like you do. No one else sees the world like you do. That is the beauty of being you. Another thing to understand is that although you are unique, you are not alone. There are a lot of other people who are going through the same kind of challenges as you. Others understand what you are going through and if you need help with your personality there are many people who can help you. Get to know yourself and your personality traits. If you want to change something about yourself then go to work on it. That is the growth process. And growth is what this life is all about. Go for it!

YOUR SELF-ESTEEM

So far we have talked a lot about you. We talked about your world, how you see yourself (your perspective) and your personality. Now we're going to get really personal. Now, we're going to talk about self-esteem. "What is self-esteem?" you might be asking. Self-esteem is not how others see you, it is how you see yourself. To make it seem a little clearer, look at self-esteem as two words: self and esteem. Esteem means to value something. If you esteem something highly, that means you feel it is very important and valuable. If you don't esteem something highly, it is of little importance or value to you. The first part of self-esteem is 'self.' In other words it is you yourself. So, self-esteem means how you value yourself. That is why it has only to do with you and not how others see you. It has to do with how much you believe you are of value and have something to offer to others.

You are the only source of your self-esteem. You can't blame it on anyone else. You can't say somebody made you like you are. A lot of self-esteem has to do with how you see yourself, how you interpret others' reactions to you, and how others interact with you. It has much to do with your perception of yourself. That is why we spent so much time in this chapter talking about perception and interpretation.

Some people don't believe they are worth very much or that they have much to offer others. This means they don't value themselves very much. This is called low self-esteem. Some people think they have a lot of value and have a lot to offer the world. This is called high self-esteem. Most of us fall somewhere in between the two extremes. We tend to feel that we have some value but there are times we don't feel good about ourselves. Our self-esteem varies, it goes up and down to a certain degree.

FAMILY AND SELF-ESTEEM

So what influences your self-esteem? Growing up in your family is the place where you learned most about who you are and how valuable you are as a person. Sometimes our families, the ones that should love and support us the most, are the source of our worst pain. This comes about for many reasons and we discuss them in more detail later. Let us just say here that our families can create a sense of worth or worthlessness in ourselves.

SOME PEOPLE (ESPECIALLY THOSE WE LOVE) SAY THE DUMBEST THINGS!

One reason many of us have insecurities is because somebody said something in our youth or adolescence, whether true or not, that stuck! This is a fairly common occurrence in our families. Brothers and sisters, mothers and fathers sometimes say things that really hurt. Sometimes they don't know it hurts. Other times they are really trying to hurt us. Either way, it hurts and many times, it sticks.

Cathy had a brother who she adored. One day, when she was 16, as she and her brother were working out, he told her in a joking brotherly way, "You sweat pretty for a fat girl." Seem like a silly harmless statement? Cathy didn't think so. She already had insecurities about her body. Even though she was not fat at all, this nonsense statement gave her a "chunky complex" throughout her high school years and into early adulthood. It affected how she dressed. She typically wore clothes to hide her figure and it wasn't until she was in her mid- to late- 20s that she realized that her body was okay.

A silly comment also affected Greta in much the same way. She was very athletic at a young age. For birthdays she would ask for bats and balls, not dolls. One night, in her impressionable teen years, she was getting ready for the evening and decided to wear make-up and tryout a purse. She came down the stairs and her family members, who were used to seeing her as a tomboy, broke out laughing. They didn't mean to hurt her feelings, but in her mind, the laughing meant, "Your sister's trying to look like someone she's not." For years after that night, she wouldn't wear make-up or a feminine haircut. It took her until she was in her early 20s to get over this inconsiderate comment.

These ridiculous comments, whether true or not, can become part of our self-concept. Think back a minute on your life. Are there any negative comments that have influenced the way you view yourself?

The opposite can be true as well. You could have parents and family who tell you positive things about yourself and encourage you throughout your life. They can influence your self-esteem for the better. But, as you may already be thinking, you can choose to believe either one. You could in fact not believe the negative things said about yourself. And you could choose not to believe the positive things about yourself. This gives you a better idea of how your self-esteem is controlled solely by you. Others have a powerful influence on you but, in the end, you are the one who chooses what to believe.

The thing about self-esteem is that those with high self-esteem aren't the ones that typically need as much help in life. They don't tend to have as many problems with relationships. They tend not to continually choose the frog types or worse, predators, who cause so much pain and anguish. One or two experiences with a frog type or a predator type guy and they learn their lesson, send the guy packing, and move on to someone who will treat them with the respect they feel they deserve.

That is not to say that girls with high self-esteem don't get hurt in relationships. They can get caught up in guys only to be mistreated or have the relationships break up. But generally speaking, the higher the self-esteem a girl has, the less likely she is to get into a bad relationship, and, if she does, the more quickly she can recover and move on with her life. Why? Because she knows that her value as a person is not tied to whether a guy accepts her or not. So she can keep going, minimizing the emotional damage of a relationship gone bad.

TALKING TO YOURSELF ABOUT YOURSELF

For those girls who don't have a very high self-esteem, the question might be asked, "How do l work on my self-esteem?" Let's look at a few things you can do to change the way you see yourself. The first thing you can do is pay attention to your self-talk. Self-talk is that little inner voice that is constantly talking to you. We all have that inner voice. For some strange reason, this inner conversation with ourselves tends to be negative. We say negative things like, "l'm such an idiot," or "How could l be so dumb?" or "l'm fat," or "l don't make friends easily." We say little sayings like these to ourselves. But we tend to focus on a handful of them. We say them over and over to ourselves, especially when things aren't going very well for us.

It often seems easier to believe the negative messages about yourself than the positive ones. It may be that the negative messages are often delivered with strong emotions, like anger, while the positive messages are more low-key, sometimes accompanied only by a simple smile, or nothing at all. Saying bad things to yourself can have a very negative effect on your body and your spirit. Negative statements tend to weaken you, both physically and spiritually. You can make yourself physically and spiritually weaker by saying negative things to yourself, or stronger by saying positive things. That's one reason why athletes say positive things to themselves and visualize themselves doing their sport perfectly.

So one of the first things you can do to increase your self-esteem is to begin changing how you talk to yourself.

SELF-ESTEEM EXERCISE NO. 1

For three days, pay attention to your inner voice conversations. Keep a small notebook with you and write down the positive comments and negative attacks you say to yourself, either out loud or in your head . Writing them down is critical to making this exercise work. Are there more negative or positive statements? The higher number will give you a pretty good idea where your self-esteem is, whether high or low. Then, ask yourself if the statement is true. In the case of the negative statements, ask yourself if there is any other way to think about the situation. There almost always is, especially when it has to do with telling yourself that you are not very good in one way or another. Now write down the other possible interpretation. Lastly write down a possible positive statement to replace the negative one. If you continue to do this, you will begin to see patterns of self-talk. You will also begin to feel more positively about yourself.

SELF-ESTEEM EXERCISE NO. 2

Another thing you can do is to ask an adult to take you under their wing, so to speak. If this adult is not one of your parents, it must be someone you can trust and preferably someone your parents know and trust as well. This may seem like a weird idea, but an adult who you respect, and who will respect you, can offer you a mature perspective to help you get through some tough times and tough choices. You are looking for someone, preferably a female, who will mentor you. A mentor is someone who takes on a young person to teach them a particular skill by example and training. That is the basis for the Big Brothers/Big Sisters organization. They match adults with kids who need an adult role model and friend. It is a very successful program, mostly because of the healthy relationship the kids build with an adult.

SELF-ESTEEM EXERCISE NO. 3

For one week say "hello" to everyone you pass by at school. All you have to do is say "Hi." You don't have to do anything else. Try this for a week or two and see if it doesn't make a change in how others treat you. It's almost guaranteed that you will have a positive experience. Saying "Hi" makes people feel good when they are around you.

SELF-ESTEEM EXERCISE NO. 4

Ask yourself the following questions then proceed to the second part of the exercise.

1.   What insecurities do I have?

2.   Which ones are a result of a comment made by someone else?

3.   Which ones are the result of how I perceive myself?

Think about the answers to the questions you asked above. Now make a list of three insecurities or statements answering the above questions. Next take a few minutes and rewrite them in a positive statement about yourself.

An example of this might be that you feel your nose is too big and you feel self-conscious about it. You could rewrite statements about your nose, something like: "My nose makes me unique. It is part of me and I am a unique and beautiful person." Or if you think that you don't make friends very easily you could write a statement like, "I am a likeable girl, and people are attracted to me by my friendly personality." Do this with each insecurity you have about yourself.

The next step feels a little strange for most people but it can be a very powerful exercise, so do it for your own good. Look into the mirror everyday and say to yourself, "I am a beautiful person of infinite worth. I will treat myself and others accordingly." This may be hard to do because you may not believe it at first. But if you continue to tell yourself this, you will begin to believe it. It may take several months of doing this daily, but it will happen. You can choose to tell yourself positive messages or you can choose negative ones. The choice is up to you. You will begin to believe whichever one you choose to tell yourself. The positive ones are closer to the real you. Believe it. Allow yourself to believe it. Tell yourself how great you are and others will begin to treat you that way.

SELF-ESTEEM EXERCISE NO. 5

Each day, write one thing positive about yourself, something that makes you feel good, something you like about you. That's all you have to do. Just one thing each day.

DISCOVERING NEW PARTS OF YOU

Discovering new talents is a great way to build your self-esteem. An important thing you can do to prepare yourself for a healthy, happy life is to develop yourself. It defines where you spend your time and who you spend your time with. If you are going to date interesting and healthy guys you need to be interesting and healthy.

Remember Princess Kate liked playing the harp and riding her horse. But she let the guys she dated take her away from those things that were really enjoyable to her. She didn't realize it until after the frog spell was cast that she had abandoned many of her interests. It didn't take her long to return to those things she liked doing, finding a great deal of enjoyment in them again.

If you feel you have no interests, or have convinced yourself you are a boring person - that is a negative perspective and doesn't serve you well. Replace those thoughts with positive ones. Stand in front of the mirror every morning and say, "I'm a great person to be around." "I'm interesting. I enjoy many things such as (recite things you enjoy in your life)." Do this every morning until you find that those negative thoughts are replaced by your new positive ones. Begin to extend yourself by trying new things, you will discover a whole new world will open up to you.

BODY TYPE

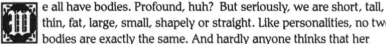 e all have bodies. Profound, huh? But seriously, we are short, tall, thin, fat, large, small, shapely or straight. Like personalities, no two bodies are exactly the same. And hardly anyone thinks that her body is as good as what she would like it to be. Everybody seems to want something different than what they have. So don't consider yourself different than everybody else just because you don't like your body or some part of it. You may want bigger or smaller breasts, a smaller or different shaped rear-end, longer or shorter legs, less body fat, longer fingers, or any number of possible changes. We could go on and on. The point is, no one is totally satisfied with her body.

There are essentially three different body types that we all fit into with some variation. They are Mesomorph, Endomorph, and Ectomorph body types. Now these may seem like big names. They are, so we will refer to them as full-figured, athletic and slender. Basically, the athletic body type is said to be relatively strong and muscular. The full-figured body type is somewhat more "rounded," sometimes considered overweight or having higher body fat. This is not always the case, however. Some full-figured body types have rather low body fat, they are still shaped somewhat round. The slender body type is long, lean and straight chested. Most people are some combination of all three types.

You had little to do with choosing your body type. That was mostly determined by your genes, your family heredity. But you have everything in the world to do with accepting your body type as being who you are.

And you shouldn't think that one or the other body types is necessarily more attractive than the others. What you will find is that different people find each body type attractive. For instance, if you look in most of the fashion magazines you would see mostly slender body types on the female models. Female models tend to be long, tall, skinny and even frail looking. This is mostly because the longer body tends to be photogenic. That is the image the magazine people are trying to sell you as ideal. However, many men wouldn't be the least bit interested in those models. And there are men who are only attracted to the full-figured type bodies.

But if you want to know the real secret to attractiveness read on. Here's the biggest secret: it is not your body type that makes you attractive, especially in the long term. What makes you attractive to others is your personality, how you treat others and how you interact with them. That's it! That's the big secret.

THE BIG SECRET

One teenage girl who read the big secret agreed but she responded with, "Somebody should tell the secret to the guys at my school." She wanted to believe the secret and she knew in her heart that it was right. But the guys in her school hadn't been let on to the secret yet. They obviously had been concentrating almost solely on looks. That's the whole point of this book. To help you understand what is really important so that you can recognize the frogboys in your world, know where they are coming from, and avoid them.

The big secret is it's true for guys as well as girls. You probably know many good-looking guys. Some are more attractive to you than others. But there are also some of them that you wouldn't go out with if you were paid to, even if they are very good looking. What's the difference between all these good-looking guys? It's their personalities, how they treat you, and how desirable you perceive them to be.

Let's look at each one of these concepts for just a moment. There are certain personality types that are attractive to you. These same personalities wouldn't be attractive to your friend and vice versa. This would be the case whether it is a guy or a girl. There are some girls you wouldn't be friends with just because you don't like or wouldn't want to hang with that personality type.

What about how they treat you? You have probably had the experience of not really noticing a particular guy, until you discover he is interested in you. Unless he is the biggest 'jerk' in the whole world you probably took a second look at this guy and found him more attractive than you had before.

In addition to this experience, you may have noticed that guys that treat you well become more interesting and often more attractive to you. The same goes for you. If you treat others with kindness, interest and concern you will be more attractive to them. This is almost always the case, no matter what body type you have.

What does this have to do with body type? We are trying to help you see that there are other things, more important than body type, that make you attractive to others. So placing a great amount of emphasis on your sense of self-worth based on your body does not serve you very well. Having said that, we understand that your perception of your body and its acceptability to you and others is very much tied to how you view yourself. That's just the way it is.

Let's do a little exercise to help you examine what you think the ideal body type is and how it compares to how you perceive your body.

THE IDEAL BODY EXERCISE

The following exercise is a list of body parts you may pay attention to. On the left side of the chart you should circle what you feel is the ideal for that body part. Only circle one choice per line/body part. On the right side of the chart you should circle how you perceive your body for each part listed. (This list may not include all the body parts you might want and the choices may not be exactly how you would describe your ideal, but they should be close enough to give you a clear choice.) After you have circled a choice for each body part on the "ideal" side and on "your body" side, you should go to the last column on the right titled 'Change' and put a check on the line of any body part you would change if you could. After you have done that we will discuss what this all means for you

What does this exercise say about you? First you need to know that there is no "ideal" body type or "ideal" for body parts. Your ideal is what you have decided or have been influenced to believe is the best way to look. This does not mean it is, in fact, the best. It simply means that you perceive it to be the ideal, which also means that you can change your perception about it being ideal. This is especially true if your perceived ideal body differs from how you see your own body.

Take a look at how many parts you circled differently from the ideal for your body. If you circled the same description for most of the body parts, what you think is ideal and how you view your body are very similar.

THE IDEAL BODY EXERCISE

Body Part	The Ideal Body			Your Body			Change
Head	Small	Medium	Large	Small	Medium	Large	☐
Hair	Thin	Full-Bodied	Thick	Thin	Full-Bodied	Thick	☐
Eyes	Blue	Green	Brown	Blue	Green	Brown	☐
Nose	Pointed	Flat	Broad	Pointed	Flat	Broad	☐
Lips	Thin	Medium	Broad	Thin	Medium	Broad	☐
Cheeks	Flat	Medium	High	Flat	Medium	High	☐
Chin	Square	Rounded	Pointed	Square	Rounded	Pointed	☐
Neck	Short	Thin	Long	Short	Thin	Long	☐
Shoulders	Slight	Straight	Wide	Slight	Straight	Wide	☐
Arms	Short	Medium	Long	Short	Medium	Long	☐
Fingers	Short	Medium	Long	Short	Medium	Long	☐
Breasts	A	B/C	D	A	B/C	D	☐
Stomach	Flat	Rounded	Bulged	Flat	Rounded	Bulged	☐
Waist	Narrow	Straight	Thick	Narrow	Straight	Thick	☐
Hips	Narrow	Medium	Wide	Narrow	Medium	Wide	☐
Buttocks	Small	Average	Big	Small	Average	Big	☐
Legs	Short	Medium	Long	Short	Medium	Long	☐
Feet	Small	Medium	Big	Small	Medium	Big	☐
Overall	Athletic	Slender	Full-Figured	Athletic	Slender	Full-Figured	☐

If there are a lot of differences from the ideal side to the your body side it means that you think your body is quite different than you think the ideal body is.

Now look at the parts you put a check by. These are parts you would change if you could. You may not have placed a check on a line that you didn't circle the same descriptor on both sides of the chart. That is OK. It means that even though you don't think that your body part is ideal you are still all right with it. If you put only one or two checks it means that either you have a nearly ideal body according to you, or that you are comfortable with your body the way that it is. Either way, that is a very good sign.

Much of your self-image has to do with your perception of the ideal and how close you come to matching that ideal. The healthiest approach to your body is that you work on adjusting your concept of the ideal to be more in line with your body. You should also consider the possibility that perhaps that particular body part may, in fact, change in the not so distant future. Remember, you are still growing, maturing and changing.

FLAWED MEDIA PERSPECTIVE

The media, magazines, books, TV, and movies influence what we believe is the ideal. If people don't fit into the mold the media presents, they often-times become insecure and feel inadequate. Teenage girls look at malnour-ished models and think, "Wow, if I could just look like that...." What the pictures neglect to show you is what happens between the camera shots. Most, if not all, of the pictures are doctored. They have been air-brushed or digitally altered to remove all imperfections and to alter the models' bodies to look exactly how the publisher wants them to look, not how the model actually looks. The models have also been heavily made up by professional makeup artists. These artists can literally change a person's appearance so they look nothing like their natural selves. Many times before modeling sessions, these models pay "diet consultants" a lot of money to actually move into their homes for weeks at a time to help them lose an unnatural amount of weight. Then, when the modeling shoot is finished, these models climb back up to a more natural, and healthy, weight.

One of the top models in the world was once said in an interview that she hardly recognized herself in the magazines because the pictures were so drastically altered. In addition, many models have anorexia and bulimia just to stay thin. A picture of the model hanging over the toilet won't make the cover page. These eating disorders are extremely dangerous and kill many women each year. Many beautiful models live very rough lives and are very dysfunc-tional. So those "ideal" models are not so ideal after all.

You may not have the most perfect body in the world. But your body is part of you. It is beautiful because it is part of you and you are beautiful. You may want to alter it in some way. That is a decision you will have to make, and one that you will have to live with. But being able to accept your body as beautiful in its present condition is important for your emotional health.

We have all known people who we would say have ideal bodies. But ask them what they think about their bodies. They seem to want something bigger or smaller or different shape. To others, their body looks awesome but not to them.

At 17, everyone thought Brenda had the "perfect" body. But Brenda didn't think so. Although her body fat content was healthy, she thought she was fat. She also thought that her breasts were too small, and that her hair was too brown. As she got older, she decided that she was going to change some things. She went on a very strict diet to lose weight. She had surgery to increase the size of her breasts, and she dyed her hair. After she made the changes, she was pleased with her body for a while. She was much more outgoing and friendly. She had a lot more dates. But after a while, she noticed that the guys that were asking her out were not really very nice and it seemed that every one of them wanted only one thing, to have her body. When she would resist or turn their advances down on dates, they often got very upset, and said things like, "Why do you think I spent all that money for dinner and a show," or "You know you want it too." She began to realize that the changes she made, while positive, weren't attracting the kind of guys she wanted to date.

Brenda thought that changing her body would make her happy by making her more attractive to guys. It ended up backfiring and she was even less satisfied with her life. What she needed to do was work on changing her perception about herself and her body rather than just changing her body.

Brenda decided that she liked eating instead of starving, so she returned to a healthy diet. She put on a few pounds, but she felt much better and she was still very much within the healthy body fat content range. She also worked with a therapist and made some great changes in the way she perceived herself.

What she found was that she had developed the expectation that girls with the ideal body could get dates with whomever they wanted. She also thought that her body defined who she was as a person. She finally came to accept two very real concepts: 1) she didn't need to be perfect, that everybody makes mistakes and they are still acceptable as humans, and 2) that there is no perfect body type nor does having a perfect body define you as a person. Once she was able to accept these two points she was much more forgiving of herself and she came to accept herself how she was. The side benefit to her new understanding was that she started dating guys that were more "real" and interested in her for who she was and not just for her body. She found these relationships to be much more enjoyable with less pressure to be perfect.

If you think you want to change something about your body, don't fall into the same trap that Brenda did. Do a little inner-self work first. Try changing the way you treat others. Try changing the way you look at yourself. Try changing what you think others want from you. Try not judging yourself or others according to standards that are unrealistic. Try being a little more flexible in your view of the world and of yourself and others. If you consciously try to make these changes, you are very likely to find that your world will change as well.

LOSING WEIGHT

If you want to lose weight, understand what it takes to do it properly in a healthy manner. Understand why you want to lose weight and determine if this is a healthy reason for losing weight. Also understand that if you don't make changes within yourself then you are very likely to gain the weight back. Many people who lose weight without making psychological changes as well gain the weight back plus more. They didn't change their life patterns and their self image. Consulting your physician is a great way to determine if your dieting method is healthy.

Some girls get the idea that being skinny is the cool thing to do. Some think that it is the way to fit in, and may use anorexia or bulimia as a means to lose or control weight. There are some high schools where if you are not anorexic or bulimic you are not part of the in-crowd. Being left out of the in-crowd can seem like the most devastating thing in the world for many high school age girls. Nothing could be further from the truth. If the in-crowd people are doing the anorexia/bulimia thing they are damaging themselves physically and emotionally.

If you find that you are caught up in one of these diseases you need to get into treatment as quickly as possible. Begin the healing process immediately. Search out a therapist who specializes in treating eating disorders. There are very good programs that specialize in treating these diseases. You can get help. You can escape the grip of these devastating diseases. Don't be ashamed that you have one of these diseases. By taking the step to get treatment you are doing something you can be proud of. You are doing something good for yourself. You are beginning the healing process. Several references are provided at the end of this chapter if you would like additional information on anorexia or bulimia.

HELP FOR PARENTS

This section is designed to help parents guide their daughters during the very challenging task of growing up, preparing for dating and eventually for marriage.

At the end of most chapters, we will have a Help For Parents section with suggestions on how you can help your daughter. This can be a good section for girls to read as well to help them relate to their parents.

Nearly all parents want what's best for their children. Some don't know what is best, and some do. All things considered, parents have a great amount of influence on teenage daughters. It may not seem like it, but it is true. You want the best for your daughter. You want her to go through life without unnecessary pain. You want her to make the right decisions about friends and boyfriends.

All girls go through significant physical, emotional and sexual changes as they reach adolescence (teenage years). These suggestions are also important for young adults. She will have many of the same needs at that stage of her life as well.

SOME SPECIFIC THINGS YOU CAN DO
TO HELP YOUR DAUGHTER

- ♕ Love her. The most important thing you can do as a parent for your teen is to love her. Let her know and see that you care about her. This may not always be the easiest thing to do because your teen may be misbehaving or seems to be pulling away from you. Don't take this as a sign that she doesn't need love, care and patience. It is in fact a sign that she wants and needs exactly that. The teen years are when she is having many struggles and much confusion. She needs the stability of a parent who loves her whether she messes up or not.

- ♕ Show empathy. Changes are part of growing up. You went through the same changes. You had similar thoughts and feelings. When dealing with your daughter, try to remember how you felt and what you went through. If you don't want your daughter to make the same mistakes you did, then tell her why you are making some of the decisions about what she can and can't do. She may still rebel against you. It's her life and she needs to learn and she may make some mistakes. If you are empathetic, telling her you understand how she feels but just want the best for her, it will make it easier for you to connect with her and to make rational decisions.

♕ Be supportive. Be there emotionally and physically when she needs you. For some of us, being there emotionally is one of the more difficult things we are faced with. Partly because of our own experiences and partly because we are afraid we don't know how to be emotionally available. Don't let her emotions and needs overwhelm you. If you don't feel that you can handle it or you notice that you are not handling it very well, seek professional help as a family or an individual. Being there for her is one of the most important things you can do.

♕ Work on positive interaction. If you have a history of negative interaction in the family, where names have been called or you have been strict in your discipline to the point where she may feel she is not a valuable person, you need to make amends and try to heal the wounds both for you and for her. She may reject you and that can be scary, but you are the adult and the one responsible to take the initiative to try to heal.

♕ Apologize, if necessary. All parents make mistakes. It is inevitable. Few parents set out to hurt their children but we all do it to a lesser or greater extent. A parental apology, when you have done something which has hurt her feelings, can be one of the most effective ways to stay in touch with your child.

♕ Be a good listener. Listen to her when she comes to you to talk. Don't always be ready with a quick response of advice. Sometimes the best thing you can do is not say anything but, "I see," or "That's interest ing," or "I'm sorry." Too often we think our children come to us for advice when all they really want to do is unload what's on their mind. As soon as you chime in with your grand tidbit of wisdom (which may not be so grand after all) they get mad or start an argument, usually ending by saying something like, "You just don't understand!" and stomping out of the room leaving you wondering what in the world just happened. Remember, if the communication lines have been open growing up, it will be easier for them to continue.

♕ Set boundaries. It is important that you set boundaries (rules and limits) for yourself and for your daughter. And most importantly, stick to your boundaries. Good healthy boundaries are based on logic and healthy functioning. If you don't know if you have good boundaries or know how to set them, read some books, or get professional help to figure it out. Teenagers need clear consistent rules by which they can learn how to navigate in the uncertain world of adolescence. They may not have their own boundaries, so they must rely on yours. Again, they will probably rebel against the limits you set, but that is part of growing up. They are at a stage where they must test the limits in order to find out how they fit and how to be in society. Those limits are largely defined by you and your family values and boundaries. Those are typically the safer limits. The more dangerous limits are set by the laws of the land that when tested can get your daughter in trouble, jail, or worse.

♛ Build up your teenager. Compliment your daughter as often as possible. Tell her you love her every chance you get, even if it makes you or her feel uncomfortable. You may not think it is doing her any good but if you keep it up, the payoff will be tremendous. A teenager (or anyone for that matter) needs to know they are loved. They need to know they belong somewhere and the most important place to belong is in the family. If they don't feel that way, they will look outside the family to places like boys, peers, or even gangs to find the feeling of belonging. Even with a strong family connection your daughter may look outside the family. This is normal and it would be helpful to you and your daughter to understand this. Remember to be flexible yet consistent.

♛ Be a friend but not a peer. It is important to be your child's friend, but how you do that is equally important. Some parents thrill at being thrown back into the excitement of teen-age years and relate to their children as if they were a teenager again, rather than as a parent. It may be difficult and confusing for kids when parents behave more like peers, then suddenly try to establish parental type rules.

If you as a parent find that you are getting into your daughter's world and enjoying her experience as much as she, it may be a sign that you are trying to "relive" your teenage years instead of taking on the parent role. If this is your situation you may need to back away a little from being so involved in your daughter's life. Be supportive, but don't participate too much. Stay close to her but realize that your role is as a parent who will support her, provide boundaries and limits, be there for her when she is hurting or when she is excited, and love her in all situations good or bad.

WHERE TO TURN FOR MORE INFORMATION

www.somethingfishy.org

Hall, Lindsey and Cohn, Leigh. *Bulimia - A Guide to Recovery*. Gurze Books, Carlsbad, California.

Hall, Lindsey and Ostroff, Monika. *Anerexia Nervosa - A Guide to Recovery*. Gurze Books, Carlsbad, California.

CHAPTER 3

THE WINDING ROAD TO DISCOVERY

he road to self-discovery is a long and winding one. There are many twists and turns that prevent us from seeing what lies ahead. We have a better chance of determining our destination if we know where we want to go. Desires and Goals have to do with what you want from life, who you want to be, what you expect to have, and what you feel you deserve. Nobody ever accomplished anything great in life without having a goal and then doing what it takes to achieve it. That goes for doing well in school, succeeding in a job, playing a musical instrument, doing well in sports, having lots of friends, and succeeding in relationships.

If you want to have anything good in your life, you must truly desire it and then work for it. It is up to you as an individual. You deserve to have the best life possible. But to have the best, you must overcome obstacles, such as your negative self-talk, and develop the self-respect and strength to persevere until you reach your goal. This is desire.

SETTING A GOAL

 nce you desire something, you have informally set a goal. That means that just by identifying something that you want to achieve you have said to yourself that you are going to work towards that end. That is a part of the goal setting process.

If you want to overcome some negative trait such as gossiping or negative self-talk or you want to improve some positive trait, such as helping others or working out consistently, you may follow this process: 1) Identify the trait you want to change or improve. 2) Write it down in the form of a positive statement as if it were already accomplished. An example would be "I treat others with respect by not gossiping about them." Or "I work out daily and can run an 8 minute mile." 3) Do the research to find out what it will take to accomplish the task. 4) Get to work on it. 5) Review your goal daily. 6) Keep track of your progress. If you have a problem gossiping, keep track of how many times a day you gossip. Then determine to do it at least one less time per day until you don't do it at all. If you want to achieve an eight-minute mile and can only run a nine-minute mile, start working out a little more each day until you get to the point where you are whittling away at the time to achieve your goal. Once you have achieved your goal, set a new goal so that you can keep improving yourself.

Most people, especially teenagers, don't actively set goals. As a result they don't usually accomplish as much as they could. Then they wonder why they aren't getting anywhere in life. Don't let life pass you by because you don't set and work to reach your goals.

In order to work on goals you must first identify what you want to achieve. At this point in your life you may not be very clear on what that might be. There are so many changes going on in your life that the direction you should take might be hazy to you. Here is an exercise that can help you identify what it is you want to achieve or at least work on right now.

DISCOVERING YOUR LIFE AMBITIONS EXERCISE

Go to a place where you can be by yourself and where you will not be interrupted for a while. Have a pencil and paper handy. You should get very quiet and relaxed. Clear your mind of distracting worries and cares for just a few moments. Sit quietly and reflect upon your life. Ask yourself, "If I could change anything about me right now what would it be?" Write down whatever comes to your mind. It may be one thing or several things. Limit it to about three items so you don't get overwhelmed by your own answers.

Next, go through the same process and ask yourself, "If I could become something or someone what or who would it be?" Again listen to yourself and write down whatever answers come to you.

Next, think about your strengths. This is a difficult thing for some people because it seems like boasting. But, if you were to sit down in a job interview and the interviewer asked you what strengths you have, you would probably have an easier time answering this because you really want the job. Now that you are in the privacy of your own thoughts, be your own interviewer and ask yourself what strengths you have? If this is still difficult, here are some things to think about:

♛   What do you do well, whether or not it's recognized by others?

♛   What do you like to do, whether you do it well or not?

♛   What personality traits do you enjoy about yourself?

♛   What compliments do you remember getting from others?

After you write down your strengths, think of 5-10 things that are very important to you in life and list them below. These may include unspoken rules in your life. Make sure to give this list sincere thought. Here are some examples to start you thinking:

♛ Mary grew up in a home where reading books was essential to life. She enjoys books and sharing what she learns with others. Mary decides that reading is something she would miss sorely, and that she enjoys being around people who share this interest. She lists reading as important to her life.

♛ Joan is an avid mountain biker and loves the outdoors. She can't imagine life without the outdoors. She lists the outdoors and out door activities as essential to her life.

♛ Becky grew up in a family that didn't communicate very well. As a result, she is determined that open communication be a part of her adult life. She likes to talk to friends about feelings, hopes and desires. She lists communication and the ability to have open discussions on her list.

♛ Julie enjoys humanitarian work. She volunteers at the homeless shelter every month. She would feel a void if this part of her life were to disappear. She adds this to her list.

Look at your list. Put a star by the five things you don't think you can live without. This will help you determine which items on your list are most important. From this you will be able to formulate a goal to work on right now in your life.

LIFE PRIORITY LIST

1 _____

2 _____

3 _____

4 _____

5 _____

6 _____

7 _____

8 _____

9 _____

10 _____

Just remember to believe in yourself. Desire to have a better life and continually work on improving yourself. You will become what you desire and work towards becoming. It may take you a while to achieve, or you may not achieve exactly what you originally desired, but you will see positive benefits from the process all along the way.

PEERS

"Tell me what company you keep and I'll tell you who you are."

—Miguel de Cervantes

 e don't just have friends. We choose our friends. The friends we choose influence us. Your friends influence how you spend your time, what you like or dislike, who you like or dislike and even what you choose to do with your life. They'll also affect the way you feel about yourself.

In short, your friends, especially during the teenage years, are one of the most powerful influences on your life. More than likely, they will have more influence on you during this time of your life than your parents, brothers and sisters, teachers, preachers or anyone else. It is important you pick friends that see your potential as a person. You don't need to do anything to "prove" you're cool. In fact, any time you have to prove something to someone, you are probably with the wrong crowd.

WHY FRIENDS ARE SO IMPORTANT

Friends give us a sense of acceptance. When others accept us, we feel like we belong. Up until you became a teenager, you should have been getting much of your sense of belonging from your family. That doesn't always happen.

Some of us don't get the acceptance and love from our family that we need. But even if you did, now in your teen years you are going to be separating a little bit from your family. It is all part of becoming an individual and your own person.

A note of caution is appropriate here. That is that even though you are feeling the need to become your own person that doesn't mean you should rebel against and/or abandon your family. If you feel like rebelling that generally comes from feeling the need to differentiate but not being allowed to do so by your family. So you feel you need to fight harder and you think the best way to do it is to rebel against anything and everything that is representative of your parents and family or authority in any form. If you feel the need to rebel, take a second look at it and see if there isn't another way to get the same thing without the negative consequences of rebellion. You don't have to rebel, you just have to know what you are trying to achieve. You are trying to become your own person.

Friends are an important part of becoming your own person. Without friends you may feel alone, worthless, and like an outcast. Why do these feelings come up? Because we all need connection. We all need to be with others. It is part of being human. It is part of you.

PICKING FRIENDS

Being part of a group is an important part of being human. But you might be wondering how to pick good friends and how to get away from those you don't want to hang around with.

It can be a little awkward to find new friends. It may feel that you are abandoning those you are friends with now. You shouldn't feel too bad about it, however. Would it surprise you to know that most people only have one or two "true friends" that they end up keeping in close contact with after high school. The many friends you have or want to have in school can perhaps be more accurately described as "good acquaintances."

There are some things that you can do to find new potential friends. One thing is to begin doing different activities or get involved with other groups. For instance, if you have been hanging out with a group that typically likes to spend time at the local mall, then stop hanging out at the mall and start going to activities with a group that does something else. There are a hundred other things, like music, student government, sports, hiking/climbing, skiing, acting, science, and many others. Each of these activities attract different types of people. You may not think that you would like the people in some of these groups, but then again, you may be surprised. Try some out. Keep in mind what your objective is. You are trying to find "new" friends. That means people who don't necessarily do the things that you do right now. So don't reject the idea of trying to befriend others just because you don't know if you will like them.

Another important thing to do to find new friends is to expand your own interests. Try out new things that you may not have considered before. Shelly was a junior in high school. She was tired of her friends because they wanted her to do things she wasn't comfortable with, like drinking and smoking. She wanted to get away from them, but they kept asking her to go with them and she didn't want to be alone, especially on the weekends. Finally, she decided that she was going to try to find some new activities to expand her interests. She decided to try to learn to make pottery. There was a pottery program at the local community center. It was a little awkward at first, because she didn't know anybody there. But she found that she liked working with clay and making things. It took her a while to get to know some of the others, but she did very well in the class and others noticed her talent and began to interact with her. She liked spending her time at the community center. When her old friends would call her and try to get her to go party with them, she would simply tell them she was already doing something else. At first they were upset at her, but she didn't let that bother her too much because she wanted to get away from them. Eventually she made some very good friends who liked doing more of the things she liked. She found that she had a lot more fun with her new friends. Shelly found new friends by expanding her own interests. You may need to do the same in order to find new friends.

Another thing to do is to go back to the self-esteem exercises in this chapter. If you didn't complete all of them, do so now. Why? Because often what keeps you from making good friends or finding new friends, and keeps you with friends who may not be very good for you is your own self-esteem. If you work on building your self-esteem you may find it easier to find the kind of friends that you want.

REJECTION

lease, tell me I'm OK. Tell me I fit in. Tell me I'm not a freak. Accept me, Please." That's what we want: to know we are not freaks. When someone doesn't include us in their world, it feels like a rejection, and we can feel bad about ourselves.

On a popular TV talk show a "look at me now" segment showed a girl behind the screen telling her story - let's call her Jenny. Jenny told of how a girl (we'll call her Beth) in high school had constantly teased her about her weight, her clothes, her hair and anything else she could come up with. Now, some years later, Jenny had lost a lot of the weight, was making great money so she had nice clothes and hair and drove a BMW. She seemed to have it all now. The reason she was on the show was to confront her tormentor, Beth, to show her how good she is now and say in essence, "You used to give me grief but look at me now and look at you. I'm so much better. In fact, I'm better than you are and you used to make fun of me. Ha Ha."

Beth was brought out. Jenny came out strutting her stuff, much to the audience's delight. The host asked Jenny to explain why she and Beth were on the show. Jenny started to explain that Beth had made fun of her in high school. As Jenny explained she choked up and tears came to her eyes. After all these years and after all the success and improvements that Jenny had made she still ached inside because of what Beth had said. All the success, BMW, money and time hadn't erased the pain Beth had caused.

Were Beth's comments true? No! Did Beth's comments mean that Jenny was any less valuable as a human being? No! Did Beth's comments hurt? Absolutely! Where did Beth's comments come from? As the show progressed it was apparent that Beth, who felt she had not made very much of herself through the years, was terribly insecure and lonely. Her attempts to make Jenny feel bad in high school had come from her own sense of insecurity and feelings of worthlessness. She was trying to make herself feel better by making someone else seem worse than she perceived herself to be. Did it work? No. All that came of it was two girls who felt miserable.

If you feel rejected by some one or some group ask yourself whether those people are really who you want to have as friends. Although it may not seem like it, there are others who are options as friends. So many times girls have tried to be included in the group who they thought were the "in" group only to discover that the group ended up hurting them.

Rejection can seem like one of the most devastating things in your life. Some of the reasons people reject others are because they are just plain mean, they have a low self-esteem themselves, they fear the unknown or they feel they are competing with the one they are rejecting. Whatever the reason for the rejection, you should understand that it says nothing about your value as a human. Does that mean it won't hurt if you do get rejected? No. It means that even with the pain of rejection, you can go on with your life, find new interests or new friends who are worthy of your friendship, and help others feel better about who they are as well as yourself.

THAT NAGGING EMPTINESS

ometimes there may be a nagging sense of emptiness in your life. You may feel like something is missing, and you can't seem to figure out why. Having some sense of emptiness or incompleteness is part of being human, and especially is part of being a teenager.

Teenage and young adult years are confusing in that it is a time when you are differentiating from your parents and family, yet yearn to turn to them for help. During your teen years is when you begin to strike out on your own and begin to understand that you are a person separate from your parents and your family. However, this can leave you feeling alone and confused as you try to make sense of it all.

FEELING YOU DON'T FIT

You may feel alienated from friends and family. You don't feel like you fit in anywhere. It may seem that you are the only one that has ever experienced feeling this way. Everybody has experienced these same feelings. They may not want to admit it, but they have. Keep working on yourself and you will eventually come to understand how you fit into your big picture. This is part of growing up.

It may seem that your problems are overwhelming. It makes it even worse when you try to talk to your parents, and even some friends, and they act like your problems are minor. Well they're not minor to you, they're major to you. Others may not be going through exactly the same things you are, but they have their own problems. Keep in mind that your problems are manageable. They may seem overwhelming but you can learn how to handle them with some hard work. Sometimes it even calls for some help from somebody else such as a real friend or a professional therapist. But most of the time you will be able to get through your problems because you are capable.

FEELING BLUE

Sometimes, you may feel "blue," or depressed. Almost every teenager does. This can come from the hormone changes going on in your body, from the sense of being unsure about your world or a combination. Short bouts of depression are normal, but if you experience prolonged depression (accompanied by difficulty sleeping or sleeping too much, changes in eating habits, difficulty being around people, or even thoughts of death) you should immediately seek help from a professional therapist.

LIVING CONSISTENTLY WITH YOURSELF

Sometimes you get a feeling of emptiness because you are not behaving the way you know in your heart you should. If you are behaving in ways that are contrary to how you have been raised, or that are different from your core beliefs and values, you will experience what is called dissonance. This means you are out of harmony with yourself. Your actions are disagreeing with your beliefs. This will almost always cause a sense of loneliness or dissatisfaction. Most people try to ignore this feeling or explain it away by telling themselves that they are "doing their own thing," or they don't really believe that. You may have found yourself doing these same kinds of things. But in reality it still causes dissonance within.

DISSATISFIED WITH PARENTS

Sometimes teenagers get a sense of emptiness because they are dissatisfied with their family or parents. Children often grow up thinking that their parents should have been different, or treated them better, or should not have done some thing or the other. If you have some of these feelings you are not alone. But that doesn't mean you are going to be messed up for the rest of your life because of your family or parents.

YOU NEED LOVE

Sometimes you get that feeling that something is missing because it is. And sometimes what you are missing is what every person needs—love and affection from the most important people in your life: your mother and father. This need does not change just because you are a teenager. But it seems that it becomes harder to get because you are struggling to be your own person.

Teenagers try to fill this space with other things such as friends, boyfriends, work, shopping, sports, music, clothes, etc. In extreme cases they turn to sex, drugs and any number of other things that can be damaging to the search for self. What they really want and need is love and care from their mother and father. So don't fool yourself into thinking that you can fill that emptiness with other things. Sometimes it just takes some reconnecting with your parents and your family or with someone who is a parental figure in your life.

FEELING ABANDONED

Another thing that can bring about that empty feeling is a sense of abandonment. Abandonment is closely related to the lack of care and love discussed above, but it is more intense. At some point in your life, you may have felt you were left alone to fend for yourself in the scary world. This brings about feelings of being less secure, being less safe in your world, and in extreme cases, feeling like no one cares about you.

Teenagers often try to get rid of the feelings of abandonment by getting into relationships. The relationship usually fills the need for companionship at first, but any sign that their partner might leave or is dissatisfied brings back all the old feelings of being abandoned. So every time something happens that challenges the security of the relationship, such as an argument or disagreement, the feelings of insecurity and being unsafe resurface. What you really need to do is take care of you and work on you by doing some of the exercises in this chapter or by seeking professional help.

DIVORCE

Having parents split up, or divorce often brings feelings of emptiness to children. Children of divorce often feel abandoned by the parent who leaves. They lose that all-important daily connection with the absent parent. They get confused, often thinking they caused the divorce, and that if they had been a better child their parents would still be together. If your parents divorced, you must understand that you had nothing to do with the divorce, even if your parents might have said something like that or tried to blame you in some way. It was not your fault. It was their decision and it was separate from you. It had nothing to do with you. Let go of it if you are holding onto those kinds of feelings so you can begin to move on with your life.

VIOLENCE AND PHYSICAL ABUSE

Violence in your family can also create feelings of emptiness. If there is violence in your family, your home may not feel safe to you. A child growing up needs safety as much as love and attention. The world can be a scary place and the only safe place to a child is with mommy and daddy. If one or both parents are violent, then the child has no safe place. The whole world seems unsafe. Some forms of physical abuse are hitting, angry spanking, whipping with a belt or stick, throwing things, restraining, or threatening to do any of these things.

EMOTIONAL ABUSE AND NAME CALLING

Being emotionally abused often brings feelings of emptiness or worthlessness. Emotional abuse happens when someone says or threatens you with something that is hurtful to you. Not every negative thing that is said about you or to you is emotional abuse. But comments like, "You'll never amount to anything," or "You're nothing," or "You're worthless," are definitely abusive because they offend your very nature. Also calling names can be very abusive. These types of verbal abuses label you as inferior, worthless, and no good. They are not true.

Many people think that a "little name calling," is OK. They are fooling themselves. Name-calling can damage your self-esteem immeasurably, but only if you let it. The problem is that as a young child you don't have the defenses to keep the name calling from hurting you.

Calling yourself names can also contribute to your feelings of emptiness. You can be a big influence on yourself and on your self-esteem. Don't say things like, "You big idiot," or "I'm so stupid," or "I'm such a klutz," or "I'm no good." Anything similar to these types of things that might be going through your head can have a negative impact on how you feel about yourself. If others say negative things about you, ask them to stop. If they continue, realize it is because they are insecure, not because you are less of a person. You may not always have control over what others say, but you do have control over your own self name calling.

SEXUAL ABUSE

Another thing that can create a sense of emptiness is sexual abuse. Sexual abuse happens when someone touches you in a sexual way. Usually this happens as a child, but sexual abuse can happen to teenagers and adults. The key is if you don't agree to be touched, or if the person touching you is much older than you, like three or more years. Even boyfriends in high school can sexually abuse you if they demand that you touch them or they touch you sexually without you wanting it.

Sexual abuse almost always creates a feeling of emptiness. Victims of sexual abuse often get mixed up about what a relationship is all about. They are very often confused and have a hard time making sense of the world. They have difficulty creating and maintaining a healthy relationship. An abuse survivor often feels like they are damaged goods so they don't think they deserve a good relationship. They then, many times, pick partners who don't treat them well and perhaps even end up abusing them again in various ways.

If you think, or you know, you have been sexually abused, the first thing you should know is that it was not your fault. You were not responsible for being abused, even if your abuser told you that you were. Second, you need to know that you are not damaged goods and you deserve the best even if someone has told you that you don't or you believe that you don't.

A girl who has survived sexual abuse definitely needs to seek professional help. The best place to get help is from a qualified professional therapist who specializes in working with survivors of sexual abuse.

These are several of the most common and most powerful causes of that feeling of emptiness some girls experience. This feeling of emptiness does not have to keep you from being happy, but very often it does. Many times it is necessary to get professional counseling in order to work through the issues and feelings associated with these feelings of emptiness. Other times you can work through them on your own if you understand what the feelings are telling you.

CONCLUSION ON SELF-DISCOVERY

 ave courage in your quest to discover yourself. It can be an exciting journey. It may be a confusing one. It is for many of us. But it will be a very rewarding one once you make it through. And you will make it through, even though at times it may not seem like it. Work on yourself. Get to know yourself before you venture too far into the dating world. Knowing who you are will save you a lot of sorrow and bring you much happiness.

Remember to keep in mind that the quest for self-discovery may be a life-long process. You may think you have figured it all out, only to have days of confusion. You may find it worthwhile to reread certain sections of this book as a reminder and to help you refocus your thoughts.

HELP FOR PARENT

Refer to this section at the end of Chapter 2 for help tips.

Chapter 4

ENTERING THE DATING SWAMP: WATCH YOUR STEP

nd from across the pond, their eyes met, locked together for a magical instant. At that moment, Kate knew that they were meant to be together. There was just one catch. He was all green and slimy and his tongue flicked in and out. Could she endure the amphibian that sat before her long enough to get to know the man inside the frog? With only a slight hesitation, she knew she could risk it. After all, he looked like all the other frogs except for those eyes that had held her spell-bound for that miraculous moment. She was a fool for nice eyes. This was a frog she wanted to get to know. He was, she fantasized, different than all the others. She figured if she was going to have to slog through a few ponds to find her prince it might as well start here. But still, there was that gnawing doubt she couldn't shake...would he feel the same way?

You may have felt like Princess Kate. You may have noticed some guy for the first time, or felt that excitement of seeing someone new who is somehow different from all the others. You want to meet him or go out with him, but you're not sure if he would feel the same way about you. And if he does, would he be a good person to go out with? Would you and he get along?

It's not easy to know how to feel. You don't know if you'll like him after you get to know him. You never know if he's going to be a frog forever or if he may in fact be a prince. You don't know how he treats women. You wonder if you'll end up getting hurt, dumped, or if things will work out for the long term. All you know is that he is very attractive and you've got butterflies in your stomach.

That's what dating should be all about: trying to figure out what kind of guy he is, what kind of guys you like, what kinds you don't like, and if he's going to treat you with kindness and respect. Or is he going to be one of those frogs that thinks mostly about himself?

Dating has different purposes depending on your age and your stage of life. When you are younger, especially in the teen years, dating should be just for fun. Your objective should be to enjoy life as much as you can, and to get to know people in different situations and settings. This may be a new experience for you. You may not know what you are doing at first. You may feel awkward, but don't worry about it too much.

It's a good idea to date for practice while you are in your teen years. Practice being social. Get to know many different people. Discover the kind of guys you like and dislike and the traits that are important to you in a guy. Date to learn how to interact with members of the opposite sex.

Even under the best of circumstances, dating can be nerve-wracking and tricky. It can be very helpful to learn some of the more critical things about dating when you're still young, before it really "counts."

DATING FOR FUN AND PRACTICE

 aving fun in life is important. And dating should be a part of the fun in life. But dating can be scary. Why? Well, there's trying to put your best foot forward and "put on a show" (or at least not embarrass yourself), and then there's the rejection which may be waiting. There are the worries about safety, being uncomfortable with someone new, getting to know someone new, having to answer a million questions about yourself and so forth.

All these concerns about dating are real. So try to take the pressure off. Date for fun. If you are dating just to have fun, to enjoy being with others, and to get to know your date, then you don't have to worry so much about what he is thinking of you. You can be yourself without pretending to be something you are not just because you think someone will like you better. If some guy likes you, great. If either of you choose to pass, that's OK too. Approaching dating in this way can make it a lot easier--and a lot more fun.

But here's the best part: when the pressure is off, the real you will come out. This makes interacting more genuine in terms of learning what you and he are really like. Don't date to try to make him your boyfriend or to see whether you want to marry him—there will be plenty of time for that in the coming years. When you take the pressure off by not asking yourself, "Is he the one?" you will have more fun, and you will enjoy his company more.

WHEN TO START DATING?

 efore you get too far into this dating thing, let's back up a little. As anxious as you might be to get started dating, you should probably not be dating one on one and spending significant time alone with just each other until you are at least 16 years old. Now if you are under 16, before you pick the book up and chuck it at the nearest fireplace, consider this: there are lots of activities that you can do with guys, such as hanging out with a group of friends, meeting at dances and enjoying get-togethers. This is a safer way to get together with guys without the pressures and problems that come with individual dating. It helps you learn how to have fun with the opposite sex without getting serious. Group dating can be a lot of fun because there are more people, more fun ideas, and different interaction options. You also make more friends, which expands your options. It's just generally a good idea.

What isn't a good idea is dating one-on-one before about 16. Why? Because as mentioned in Chapter 2, there are changes that start to occur in most teenage girls right about age 16. Your body and your mind change dramatically. Before 16, getting serious about dating leads to a lot of problems. This is especially true if you are one of those girls that has matured early (all your parts were shipped express delivery). What usually happens is that older guys get interested in you, and it feels great to be noticed by and attractive to older guys. But these older guys have been around awhile and have things on their minds other than just having fun. You may think this is what you want too, but it almost always leads to you getting taken advantage of and hurt.

It's ultimately your choice, along with your parents, but the reason you are reading this book is to get more clarity and understanding about the murky bog of the dating world. Sometimes what creates the bog is getting too involved, too early. So if you would take a little caring advice, just do group type activities until you are 16 years old. You won't regret waiting, but you might regret not waiting.

GOING FROM ACQUAINTANCE TO DATE

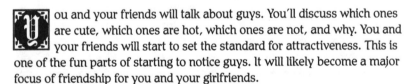 ou and your friends will talk about guys. You'll discuss which ones are cute, which ones are hot, which ones are not, and why. You and your friends will start to set the standard for attractiveness. This is one of the fun parts of starting to notice guys. It will likely become a major focus of friendship for you and your girlfriends.

You may notice that some of the guys your friends think are cute you don't find attractive and vice versa. This is due to your individual tastes—this is how it should be.

WHAT MAKES YOU LOOK TWICE?

This is where you discover that your friends have an influence on what is attractive to you but not completely. What do you look at when you first notice a guy? His eyes, his body, his muscles, his hair? Some look at the entire package then start to notice individual parts. Erin thinks that if he doesn't have a nice smile, then there is no way he can have a good personality. Jennifer notices how a guy dresses. She thinks that how a guy dresses says a lot about what he thinks of himself and how he is going to take care of himself. If he wears a black jacket, she would likely assume he's a tough guy. If he wears polo shirts she assumes he is a "preppy." Nellie has learned that she hates it when a guy is shorter than she is (she feels uncomfortable being with a short guy on a date), so she doesn't even look once let alone twice if a guy is shorter than she is. Have you ever paid attention to what it is you pay attention to? You ought to do that. Figure out what it is that you like then you can be more aware of your own likes and dislikes.

You've probably also noticed that even if a guy gets a second look, and a third or more, if after you get to know him, his personality is froggy, then you're not likely to stick around. Just the opposite may be true. He may not be the physical man of your dreams, but after you know him, you may want him to stick around. This has to do with personality being more important than looks as was discussed in Chapter 2.

GETTING A GUY TO TAKE NOTICE

Once you notice a particular guy that you think is worth getting to know better, you will need to do something to get his attention. There are many ways you and your friends will devise to accomplish this. Some will work better than others. Some will not work at all. One thing that is probably the most confusing and frustrating for girls is how to get that certain guy to notice them.

One of the biggest complaints of teen girls is that they can't get the guys they want to ask them out. They endure guys asking them out who they have no interest in. Part of the problem here is that the girls may be trying to attract the attention of the wrong guy. They are essentially chasing a fantasy about a guy who isn't for them in the first place. And while they are caught up in a fantasy chase, they may be ignoring all the signals they are getting from the guys who could actually end up being princes.

Would it surprise you to know that guys have the same fears and worries about meeting and dating girls that you do? In fact, they may have more fear because, even in today's more equal society where it is OK for girls to ask guys out, it is still expected that the guy is going to do most of the asking out. This puts most of the pressure on him. He stands to lose the most. He is the one sticking his neck out. What if she says, "No"? What if she says, "Yes"? Then what? You may experience some of the fears of rejection or the responsibility of acceptance, but the guy still takes on the majority of the personal risk when going from being an acquaintance to going on a date with you. But what can you do to get that guy's attention and let him know that you have some interest? It's a simple answer, but that doesn't mean it's easy.

The answer is called Flirting.

See. It is a simple answer. Just one word, in fact.

Now let's look at the complex part: What is flirting?

When you flirt you interact with a guy in a way that is playful and non-serious. In essence, you are playing together in much the same way little kids play but the message is different. When you were a kid the message was, "I like to play with you and it is fun." Now that you are older, the message is one of interest. You are saying, "I might be interested in getting to know you better, but I want to be playful for a while to see if you're interested too." By being playful you keep it on a non-threatening, fun level, so that if he isn't interested it won't injure your ego as much.

Flirting can be confusing because the message being sent out by you is not verbal so it has to be interpreted by the guy. He may not be very good at getting the message or taking a hint. He may miss it completely, or he may automatically think you totally want him and either go after you too quickly or run from you without giving you a chance. You probably don't want either response. The trick is to flirt in a way that the message isn't so strong that it seems like you want him so badly you might "pop." This is especially true when you are so attracted to a guy that you feel like you will pop. What's a girl to do? How do you go about flirting without seeming too serious or even desperate?

Let's look at some ideas.

A pretty effective way to be non-serious with a guy is to be funny. Make jokes. See if he laughs, even a little bit. If he and you connect on a humorous level, then that is a good sign that you may see the world in similar ways.

Another way to interact with a guy you have interest in is to tease with him a little. This means interacting with him in a playful way as opposed to teasing him by being sexually suggestive. Most guys are pretty responsive to teasing. Be careful though, guys tease differently than girls. He may respond and if he doesn't know that you are flirting with him he may see the teasing as a challenge. Then he will use his manly experience and tease you back, only his response may be a little harsh, insulting or mean. You may find that his teases make you uncomfortable. If so, you have a couple of choices to make: 1) you can either leave him alone and chalk one up to the frog category, or 2) you can change flirting tactics.

Another great idea is to make eye contact with the guy you're interested in. That doesn't mean staring at him. But when his eyes and yours meet, hold contact for a second or two. Then look away. That is intriguing to most guys and it is usually interpreted as "I find you attractive." It's also flattering to a guy to have someone take notice of him.

Another thing that guys love is to get compliments. Tell them something that you have noticed about them that is unique or positive. Keep it positive and sincere. Insincere compliments will sound manipulative or forced. Compliments on their hair, eyes, smile, muscles, clothes, intelligence, wit, accomplishments, all have a good chance of going over well if sincere.

You might want to try to get involved in activities with him, such as the ski club, acting groups, student government, or any other activity that gives you the chance to interact. This is one of the best ways to get to know a guy. You can flirt with him during these activities or just be yourself and show him some attention that indicates that you have some interest in him.

An age-old tactic, one you have probably already used, is to get a friend to approach the guy you're interested in and ask him if he has any interest in you. This is a little more forward than some other approaches but it is very effective for getting feedback about whether he is interested or not without having to put your neck out there too far. This can be an advantageous way to work it, because all guys are flattered when they find out someone is interested in them. It's a big boost to their all-important ego.

An even more direct approach is to approach him yourself. Granted, this is the riskiest approach, but it can be very effective if done right. It takes a lot of guts. He could totally reject you. Or he could also be totally interested. What you do is muster up all your courage, forget about your pounding heart, your sweaty palms, your dry mouth. You walk up to him and say, "Hi, I'm Amy." (That is assuming your name is Amy. Use your own name otherwise.) If he already knows your name, you can skip that part. Then, you ask or mention something about him. You could say that you have noticed him and wanted to introduce yourself. You could compliment him on his nice smile or the clothes he wears or how well he did in the last football game. Then see how he reacts. If he is worth half his salt, he'll be polite and start a conversation with you. (If he is shy, he may have a hard time talking with you. Don't mistake this for a rejection.) If he's a frog, he may say something rude or act rudely. If he does that, keep in mind it is not a statement about who you are. It is exposing his own lack of common courtesy. You don't want to be with a guy that acts like that anyway. If he responds positively and engages you in a conversation, then your on your way to getting to know him. If he is rude, you have just found out you don't want to waste your time and effort anyway. In either case you have been successful!

Amy, in fact, did try this approach and was very successful. She had noticed a guy in the study area that she thought was good looking. He studied in the same place almost every day. She made a point to walk by him whenever she saw him studying. She really wanted to meet him but he didn't seem to have noticed her. So she got her courage up one day and introduced herself. He was very flattered. He introduced himself and asked her if she would like to sit down and study by him. She did and in between reading pages they had a very nice conversation. They talked about where each was from, what they were studying, how school was going, and what teachers they had. They didn't make a date to go out that first day, but eventually he did ask her out and they dated each other for quite a while after that.

With all this playful interaction going on it can seem like a big game. Going back and forth, wondering what each other is thinking or what to try next. Wondering who's going to make the next move. That's probably where the term the "dating game" came from. But beware the game playing. You want to be playful and fun to be around, but don't play games. Don't show interest then when he shows interest back act like you are not interested. People usually do this because they don't want to seem too forward. Some call this playing hard to get, which supposedly makes the hard to get person seem even more attractive. This works sometimes but more often than not it backfires and the guy just thinks you're inattentive and turns his attention to somebody else.

SOME THINGS YOU DON'T WANT TO DO

Flirting is different than being a "flirt." A "flirt" is a label that often gets placed on a girl who interacts with guys in a way that sends the message "if you want me you can have me," but then rejects the guy when he responds to her. This is a double message that gets guys confused and mad, and they begin to label them with all kinds of terms we don't even want to get in to. Here are some things you should avoid doing because of the negative message they send.

- ♛ Don't be too sexual or offer yourself sexually.

- ♛ Don't be too obvious to the point of being pushy or obnoxious.

♛ Don't be too aggressive (like throwing yourself at them- this turns most guys off).

♛ Don't be cutesie in a little girl way. Acting this way gets rapidly annoying.

♛ Don't be negative. Talking about things, people, or events in a negative way is gossipy and sets a tone for the relationship. Do you really want to be in a negatively based relationship? Not many people do.

♛ Don't whine. Whining is negative, complaining, and it grates on others' nerves. This is especially ineffective if you are trying to flirt with some guy to attract his attention.

MUTUAL ATTRACTION

Sometimes you will find that you don't have to do much to attract his attention. Sometimes it just works. One of the great things that can happen is when you find someone who you are attracted to and who likes you in return. This is called mutual attraction. He likes you and you like him. There is a certain rush of confidence and excitement when this happens. It's exciting to find someone that thinks you have an attractive personality, and finds you good looking. Its great to have someone else pay attention to you and someone who wants to spend time with you. This can be very reinforcing and encouraging. It's a great feeling.

Mutual attraction begins the process of getting to know a guy on a different level than when you were just casually interacting. This gives you the chance to work on the beginnings of building a relationship by learning how to act, learning about this guy, and learning how to connect with him. You can do things like write notes to each other, call each other on the phone, send e-mails, meet between classes, talk in the hall at school. These interactions confirm your interest in each other and test the level of interest. It's one of the best parts of dating.

ONE-SIDED ATTRACTION

You will find that in many cases you are attracted to someone who either doesn't know you exist or who doesn't know he's interested. This may be the case in the majority of initial attractions. It is almost always the case that one person is attracted to the other before the other realizes it. You may think he is the most incredible thing in the world or you may just think he seems interesting and would be someone you would like to know better. Either way, one-sided attraction is a bit more awkward than mutual attraction. You are less sure whether you should risk putting yourself out there for fear of being rejected. It is more difficult to know how much effort to put out to see if he is interested at all.

Sarah was walking down the sidewalk one day and saw a guy who she thought was the best looking thing in the world. She said he looked exactly like a certain popular movie star. She couldn't wait to see him each day. She would go out of her way to get a glimpse of him. She was totally infatuated with him. The only catch was that he didn't know she existed. This was definitely a case of one-sided attraction. Not that Sarah wasn't good looking or that he wouldn't have been interested in her if he would have known her. It was just that he didn't know her and Sarah didn't have the guts to go up and introduce herself. She wasn't willing to put herself out there. So all she could do was dream about him. You may find yourself in a similar situation, you can either dream like Sarah, or act upon your feelings.

CRUSHES

One of the great dangers of dating is finding yourself so attracted to a person that your feelings overwhelm your better judgment. This is a crush. You are so totally engrossed by some guy that you can't think of anything else. You can't wait to see him. You let other things in your life take second place. But, usually a crush is one of those one-sided attractions we talked about earlier. Once the attraction becomes mutual, it is no longer really a crush but may move to an infatuation. Sarah in our previous example had a total crush on that celebrity look-alike guy she saw at school. He had no idea that she existed let alone that she was interested in him. Now if she would have had the guts to introduce herself to him and he was taken by her as well then they would have been infatuated with each other. But just being enamored with somebody is a crush.

Crushes are not logical. They come more from your belief about who he is, or an expectation about what you think he will give you, or what you can get from him, rather than from the reality of what he will contribute to a wholesome relationship. The person you have a crush on becomes almost an illusion. A line in the modern Sabrina movie warned, "Illusions are dangerous people, they have no flaws." Keep in mind, no one is perfect, even Mr. Perfect.

Most people will or have had a crush on someone. Just know that crushes are passing fancies. They are not dangerous. They are not a problem. The only possible problem could be if you start harassing the guy and he doesn't want anything to do with you. That gets into a whole different area of functioning. Don't let it get there. If you are well grounded and comfortable with yourself as was discussed in Chapter 2, you should not have a problem with that kind of behavior. So don't worry about it if you have a crush on some guy.

ASKING OUT

Asking a guy out is one way to see if he might be interested too. For the past several thousand years, only males were allowed to "make the first move" (unless marriages were arranged by parents). If guys were attracted to girls, they made their wishes known. Girls generally had to wait and hope the person they were attracted to would make the move toward them. That has all changed. It is now acceptable in most areas of the United States for girls to ask guys out for dates. This is a big shift. So take advantage of the age in which you live. Exercise your freedoms. If you are attracted to someone, ask him out. You don't have to wait for him anymore.

Asking a guy out can be a nerve-racking experience. What if he turns you down? What if he doesn't even know who you are? What if you get so nervous that you make a fool of yourself? These are all common concerns. One of the safest things you can do is to get to know the guy before you make the leap to asking out. Even if you do get turned down, it is not the end of the world. You won't die. You won't shrivel up and blow away in the next strong wind. Guys go through it every time they ask a girl out for the first time as well. Now you will get some idea of just what a guy goes through to get a date with you and perhaps you will have a little more sympathy the next time someone asks you out.

HOW DO I KNOW IF HE'S INTERESTED?

 he following are some signs that you can look for to see if that cute guy you've been flirting with actually has some interest in you.

- ♕ He talks to you
- ♕ He interacts with you when you talk to him
- ♕ He smiles at you
- ♕ He says "Hi" in the halls at school or when you see him elsewhere
- ♕ You see him glancing at you from across the way

- ♛ He walks by your locker
- ♛ He drives by your house
- ♛ He's going out of his way to be where you might be
- ♛ He offers to help with something
- ♛ He asks your friends about you
- ♛ He flirts back
- ♛ He asks you out

These are just a few of the signs he might be interested too. It is easy to misread them however. Sometimes a guy is just trying to be nice, and has no dating intentions. If you are having a difficult time figuring out his real intentions, talk to him about it. Be brave.

WHY DO GUYS ACT LIKE THEY DO?

y this time in your life, you're probably wondering what makes guys tick. Let's face it, guys and girls are different and many people have spent years trying to figure out those differences. Guys can be so confusing. One minute they seem interested, the next they act like you don't even exist. They ask you out, and then treat you like they don't remember going out with you. They ask you out and treat you like a million dollars and then laugh or snicker with the guys if they see you, especially if you and he got a little too intimate on your date. One minute he makes you feel like you're the only girl in the world. The next minute you see him laughing with some other girl. How do you make sense of it all?

The bottom line is that girls think guys are a mystery and guys think girls are too. You may never understand guys, but if you understand some things about guys it may help you keep things in perspective.

Guys and girls grow up differently, and you could say they grow up in different cultures, even if they are in the same family. How can this be? We raise girls and guys differently, even within the same families. There are certain differences that occur on a conscious and unconscious level with girls and guys, most of which is unconscious. Guys are raised to be competitive. They are taught to win, sometimes at all costs. And if he loses an argument or a fight, he feels less of a person. Part of what makes this competitive nature work is that guys have different hormones (or a different mix of hormones) running through their body. These hormones make most of the differences between girls and guys. The hormones that guys have (mainly testosterone) make them more aggressive and grow larger than girls. They make them grow bigger muscles. They make them think differently. So, in a way, a guy acting tough or distant or competitive is just a guy being a guy. That does not excuse mean or rude behavior, because he should always be able to control his behavior. But it may give you some idea about why they are acting the way they do.

Women, too, are competitive but in a different way. They compete to have relationships. Girls are raised to make connections with others (both male and female) and to be nurturing. They tend to be more sensitive and emotional than guys, especially than teenage guys. This too is tied closely to the hormones. While guys have a need to win and be one-up on other guys, girls have a need to be in a relationship. Many times girls don't feel complete unless they are in a relationship. This is important to understand when you start to feel like something is missing and you are getting a little desperate to have a boyfriend. Work on yourself first, then when you want a relationship it won't be to fill a void.

Understanding that hormones and winning are important parts of what it means to be a guy, it may be easier to understand why they need to look strong and cool. They have to win! That is why so many guys are heavily into sports. They get a great sense of value from being involved in an activity that lets them compete, shows strength and gives them a chance to win. A guy may see losing as contrary to winning and that crying and showing emotion are weak and not what boys do. So a guy will do whatever he needs to in order to avoid looking weak. Some guys will act tough or like a bully. Some will argue, pick fights, raise their voice, and display many other outwardly aggressive behaviors as a way to establish their position and strength.

Sometimes, a guy may act aloof, uninterested, stand-offish, hard to get. He may not make the first move after a date to approach you. After all, approaching you first might mean he likes you more than you like him. If that were the case, and he approached you and you rejected him in some way, then he would lose. That would make him weak. He would not be much of a man if he is weak. How can he afford to do that? In his mind, he can't. Keep in mind that most of this is played out on an unconscious level for a guy.

Girls expect strength in a guy too. Girls tend to like to be with someone who is strong and powerful. It indicates the guy will protect and provide for her. This is not to say that girls are weak and need to be protected, or provided for. Historically, men have been the provider, the protector and physically stronger sex. Women have been the nurturers, the caretakers, the home-maker and bearer of children with a special connection to their children because of that. Just as guys have been raised to be competitive and strong, girls have been raised to be nurturing. That is in large part why the captain of the football team is so admirable. He represents strength and being a dominant male. A girl who can win the dominant male is essentially assuring herself, at least on an unconscious level, of survival.

Have you ever noticed how the captain of the football team goes after the "best looking" or "most popular" girl in school? It represents winning and being the strongest provider. It means being a better man than the other guys on the team or in school. That is also why some girls don't drop a guy that is strong, but is abusive in some way. She still sees his strength as desirable for her survival, even if it means she has to put up with some abuse to have him. It may not seem to make sense, but relationships are not always very logical.

In our society, we value strength in men and nurturing in women. Those two traits are complementary. They can work well together. They can create a very fulfilling relationship. It is when a man uses his strength to dominate a woman and a woman mistakes nurturing for being submissive that the problems begin. Men get abusive and women get abused. Women try to stand up for themselves yet maintain the relationship, and men can't stand to be confronted where they may lose. So they abuse more to regain their sense of manhood by winning. It can be a horrible cycle unless you either break the cycle or get out of the relationship. If you are in an abusive relationship, get out, no matter how much you think you love him.

But sometimes girls make it hard for guys. While girls expect their guys to be strong, at the same time they wish they were nurturing too. This creates confusion in a guy because they are doing all they can to be strong. So the request to be strong and nurturing creates a dilemma. If they try to be more nurturing they then may seem weaker. So by being more nurturing, the woman may sense that he is not as strong as she wants so she finds him less desirable because he is not strong enough. So then he is confused as to how he should act around girls. It's quite a complex and confusing mess for both the guy and the girl.

The other problem is that certain hormones in teenagers are just being turned on in their bodies. They are beginning to feel the power both physically and emotionally. Most teenage guys have no idea that they are being total frogs. Just like the guys in Princess Kate's Kingdom, they think they are being normal. Some guys will begin to figure it out and make changes, controlling the hormones and treating their girls with less competitiveness and more equality. Some guys just go through life thinking they have to win at all costs, with whomever they associate (including their girl-friends and wife), and a loss of any sort is seen as meaning they are not good enough as a man.

Real men, or princes, begin to realize that winning isn't everything and that working with a woman can bring them much more satisfaction and pleasure than competing with her. They work towards accepting themselves as valu-able whether they win or not. They work on being more nurturing and caring towards others, especially their girlfriend and, later, their wife. Men with high self-esteem and self-respect don't have to compete in a relationship to feel they are OK. Men that are insecure and afraid do.

It is very confusing and it may not make complete sense about why guys are like they are. The most important thing you can do is to take care of yourself, understand where guys are coming from, and demand the best treatment from the guys you date. Don't be afraid to dump a frog you are dating if he doesn't treat you well, or if he acts like you are his property because he "won" you. There is more than just one frog in the pond and one of them will turn out to be your prince. He may not be in the pond you are presently looking in. It will probably be some future pond, but you will find one that will be worthy of you and your affection, and one who treats you accordingly.

WHAT TO DO NOW YOU'VE GOT HIS ATTENTION?

ow that you understand guys a little better, you may be wondering what to do on dates to see if he is a frog or not. The purpose of dating is to have fun and, at the same time, to get to know the per-son you are spending a few hours with. The best dating activities are those which allow you the chance to talk and/or interact with him. Activities in which there is little chance to talk or interact, like movies, don't really help you get to know each other. As you plan these dates, or if he asks you what you would like to do, it's important that you find activities that both of you think will be fun but that are interactive as well. (If you can't find an activity that both of you think will be fun, that might be an indication that you are not going to have similar interests and it may be a short relationship. Give it a try. One date is all you have at stake.)

RECOMMENDED DATING ACTIVITIES

Here are some dating ideas that are more likely to help you learn who your date is. Some of these ideas may not seem all that exciting to you, but you can pick and choose. Be creative and do different things so you can experience your dates in a variety of situations. You'll learn an awful lot about guys and maybe even something about yourself if you try different activities.

- ♛ Get together with friends and play games - This is like group dating. It can be a great way to get to know each other and still have other people to interact with, especially if you find that you and your date don't particularly hit it off.

- ♛ Go out to dinner - Less formal restaurants typically are better because the atmosphere seems to be more conducive to talking. The cost is a little less too so the pocket-book pain is less.

- ♛ Eat a picnic - Eating outside almost always sets a fun tone for the date. It tends to relax you and sets you at ease so that you can talk more easily.

- ♛ Go dancing - Dancing is a fun activity and in between songs you can talk and get to know each other. It's a good way to see his moves. But be careful not to judge him solely on whether he is a good dancer or not. A lot of frogs can dance up a storm, and a lot of princes were born with two left feet.

- ♛ Go to amusement parks or carnivals - These can be a lot of fun because there are so many activities and rides to go on.

- ♛ Drive to see autumn leaves - Drives to see things are great for getting to know each other. They can be tailored for any amount of time. They don't cost an arm and a leg. When you get there, if it is a pretty sight, it will give the two of you something positive that you have shared together.

- ♛ Participatory Sports - playing a game together is usually an easier way to get to know your date than just watching a sport. Try sports such as tennis, racquetball, bowling, golf, or any other activity that you both enjoy or that you might like to try.

- ♛ Go to events - Festivals, celebrations, football, basketball, soccer games, etc. Shared activities such as these can provide you with fond memories of time spent together.

A few more ideas include:

- Go to a bookstore and read your favorite children's book to each other

- Take bike rides

- Go hiking

- Take a swing in a batting cage

- Drive on a go cart track

- Go water skiing

- Go swimming

- River rafting

- Go miniature golfing

- Visit the local animal shelter

- Go to museums

- Do some humanitarian good deed together

The above activities are provide an opportunity for you to get to know each other.

DATING ACTIVITIES NOT RECOMMENDED

Since the purpose of initial dating is to get to know the person you are spending the day or evening with, it makes sense to do things that help make that happen. The activities listed above are examples of activities that should work for getting to know each other initially. There are however, dating activities that don't allow for much interaction and therefore aren't highly recommended for the first few dates and especially not the first date. The following are a few examples.

- Don't go to see movies in a theater, at least not on the first date. Going to movies is one of the most common activities for dates. It is also one of the most useless for getting to know your date. You both sit looking away from each other without speaking for at least 90 minutes. On the typical "dinner and a movie" date, you only get to know him when you get to sit down and eat together. Movies are great for entertainment, but in order to turn a movie into an interactive activity it should serve as the beginning point of a discussion about the movie, what you liked about it, what you didn't like about it, and other aspects of the plot and characters. If the movie is used in this way it can be a great way to spend your time on a date. However, about as deep as most people go in discussing a movie is to ask each other if they liked it or not. If a movie is all you do on your date, it may be a wasted chance to understand a potentially wonderful person.

♛ Don't go to concerts where you can't speak to each other due to the loudness of the music or because silence is required. Not that concerts are bad. They're actually usually very fun and enjoyable especially if it's a group that you are into. Again, the point is that you spend a couple hours with a guy and you hardly speak at all. On the other hand, if a guy asks you to go to a concert and it's a group you really love and totally want to see, you're probably not going to turn him down. If the only reason you go out with him is to see the concert, and not because you have any interest in him, how about having some mercy on the poor guy and being honest with him. If he still says he would like to take you then, by all means, have a great time.

♛ Avoid raves or other party activities which make it hard to speak to each other. Ditto on the reasons mentioned above.

♛ Although watching videos at a home is better than at the theater, the same holds true as far as being able to talk to each other. It may not be quite as bad as a theater because you can be more interactive in someone's home, but don't use it as a way just to pass the time.

GROUP DATING

 roup dating means that you go to the activity in the company of at least one other couple. This also includes hanging out with a bunch of friends of both sexes and just having a good time. GROUP DATING IS A WONDERFUL IDEA.

As a teenager, group dating is one of the best ways to go about dating. Group dating generally removes a lot of the "pressure to perform." You're not always in the spotlight. You can be yourself and don't always have to try to put your best foot forward. Neither do the guys. You can see each other more for who you are. You get to know each other on a real level and you can more easily see past the froggy exterior to know whether you like him or not.

Group dating brings more people into conversations. You and your date don't have to carry the conversation alone. It also makes it less likely that you will be pressured to engage in physical contact or sexuality you may not want.

BUILDING FRIENDSHIPS WITH THE OPPOSITE SEX

Building and keeping healthy, non-romantic friendships with guys can be a very important part of learning what you like and don't like in a guy. When you build friendships, you get to know the guy on a whole different level. Sometimes you will be able to engage in conversations where you learn a lot about how guys think and feel about relationships that would have taken you years to figure out by dating.

Friendships with guys that are free of the pressure of romance allows you to interact freely. You can be your true self without worrying about "being on your best behavior," so to speak. You have more fun. You feel more relaxed. Both of you are able to just be yourselves. If you find you don't like being with them, you can stop hanging out with them without the heartache of breaking up.

Sometimes, the best boyfriends are those who were friends first. You tend to know each other better on a "real" level because as friends you weren't as worried about putting your best foot forward and could just be yourself.

Being friends with the opposite sex is a good idea.

SOME DATING THINGS TO CONSIDER

 here are some things you may want to consider while you're wading through the dating swamp.

TELL ME WHY I'M DATING AGAIN?

One 16-year-old was convinced that if she didn't have a boyfriend or was not scheduled for a date every weekend, she was a failure as a person. This feeling is all too common among young people. Unfortunately, what this belief often leads to is girls accepting "desperation" dates in order to avoid loneliness. Not to be repetitive, but YOU ARE OK ALONE. And unless you really come to believe this, the chances are good that you will never have a relationship that will "fill" the emptiness you feel inside. If you want to have fun by dating, do it. But be very careful about dating in order to fill up the loneliness.

DATING SERIOUSLY BEFORE DATING GETS SERIOUS

Too many teenagers get serious with just one person and they end up dating this person throughout their fun teenage years. It probably feels good to be "with" someone, to have someone special. It's convenient to know who you are going to the school dance with. It's nice to know that you are going to have a date come Friday night.

However, almost without exception, teenaged girls who go steady with a guy, even if they marry him, end up thinking back and wishing they had done more or had more experiences. If a girl gets married before 19 years old the probability for divorce is high. In fact, up until about 23 years old the incidence of divorce is much higher than for getting married after 23. Part of this high divorce rate is due to the immaturity of the couple. Part of it is due to the fact that you need to go through the developmental stage of becoming an adult which occurs at about 20 years old. If you marry before then, at some point you are going to feel a need to go through that stage of development and it will likely cause conflict within you and within the marriage.

Another problem with going steady with one guy as a teenager is that you often become sexually active or at least experiment with each other. The result is doing adult activities (sex) with adult consequences (pregnancy) before you are emotionally, psychologically, or financially prepared to handle it. Even if you are on birth control, it is still possible to get pregnant or to contract sexually transmitted diseases. In addition, other complications can arise which you are not ready to handle. The emotional, psychological and physical issues of having sex are too difficult to deal with at this young age. These same issues are just as difficult for most males to handle at this age. Sometimes guys get away with less consequences because the girl is the one who gets pregnant and the guy just walks away. This is not right, but it is often how things go.

Going steady can seem very cool, but it can lead to a lot of problems you may avoid by dating a variety of guys. Also, dating a variety of guys will help you better know what you want in a prince when the dating gets serious. Consider it.

WHAT DO YOU WANT IN A PRINCE?

 ou've been dating quite a few guys over the past few years. Or maybe you haven't dated much. Either way, at some point you're going to have to get a firm idea of the kind of guy that you want. You're going to need to make it very clear, at least as clear as you can, what traits are important to you in a Prince. Otherwise, you will be left to whatever seems good or attractive at the time. The more aware you are of the traits you do and don't want in a guy, the more likely you are to recognize him when you see him. You'll know what guys you want to spend more or less time with and, most importantly, you'll know why.

THE "LIST"

 good way to start figuring out what you want in a guy is by making the infamous "list." If you haven't heard about the list, then fasten your seat belts because you're going to find out fast. In the spaces below or on a separate sheet of paper, list the character traits of a guy you would be interested in. Notice we did not say physical characteristics. Remember, the guys in Princess Kate's quest all looked exactly alike...and it wasn't tall, dark and handsome...in fact, it was squatty, mottled green and warty. The whole point of the wizard's spell was so that Kate and the other girls in the kingdom would have to get to know the boys for who they are, and not for what they seem to be, or what the girls fantasized them to be. Physical attraction changes over time, and in long-term relationships, the physical attraction becomes less important than how the relationship is going or how you are treating each other. You may think a guy is totally hot, but if after getting to know him he treats you like yesterday's grub, he may not seem that hot after all.

The reality is that you were probably attracted to each other physically first. That is part of why you got together. In some cases that is the only foundation for the relationship. But that is not what makes a long-term relationship fulfilling and satisfying. It's the personality traits, how you treat each other, and how your expectations are met on an ongoing basis that makes a relationship last.

So when considering traits that are important in a guy, you can list physical characteristics, but remember that they are not the only thing and are definitely not his most important traits. So, back to the character traits. Take a few minutes and list those which are most important to you:

WHAT KIND OF TRAITS IN A GUY ARE ATTRACTIVE TO YOU?

Think about the character traits of the guys you have been attracted to or have enjoyed dating. If you are having trouble recalling what they were like on your own, refer to the Personality Chart on page 40.

Now, in the left column in the chart below write the traits that you identified from the questions above, the Personality Chart on page 40, or from any other source, that are important or interesting to you in a guy. Then write a short explanation why they are important in the right column.

TRAIT QUIZ

When you look at a guy, what is the first thing you usually notice?

_____

What is the second thing you notice?

_____

After you get to know someone, what keeps you interested in him?

_____

Is a sense of humor, being able to laugh with a person important?

Yes ☐   No ☐

Why_____

Is being a little hard to figure out interesting to you?

Yes ☐   No ☐

Why_____

Is a nice smile important?

Yes ☐   No ☐

Why_____

Is it important how he treats others or just how he treats you?

Others ☐   Me ☐

Why_____

Is it important that he is kind to and good around children?

Yes ☐   No ☐

Why_____

Is the way his family interacts important?

Yes ☐   No ☐

Why_____

Is it important how he treats his parents?

Yes ☐   No ☐

Why_____

Is it important how he treats his brothers and sisters?

Yes ☐   No ☐

Why_____

Is his religion an important trait?

Yes ☐   No ☐

Why_____

Is intelligence important?

Yes ☐   No ☐

Why_____

What goals would be important for him to have?

_____

Is the type of work he does important?

Yes ☐   No ☐

Why_____

This is a good start on the list of characteristics that will help define the guys you are attracted to and the type of traits that your prince will need to have. Don't be surprised if you find that over time, some traits become less important and some traits may drop off your list all together. As you begin to focus on the traits that you listed above, you may discover that you date a guy that has that trait and it wasn't very important after all. You can either take that trait off your list, or you can alter the way you think about the trait. You can also list traits in order of importance and a trait may go down or up in relative importance. You may also find out as you mature that other traits become more important or move higher on the priority list. That's just the way it goes. Life is changing and flexible. You need to be as well.

IMPORTANT TRAITS

Important Trait   Why It's Important

_____   _____

_____   _____

_____   _____

_____   _____

_____   _____

_____   _____

_____   _____

_____   _____

FINDING THE RIGHT TYPE OF GUY

Now that you have a better idea of what you are looking for in a guy, you may be having some difficulty actually finding a guy that meets all those requirements. If you have decided to really pursue your prince but are having trouble meeting him, you might have to do one thing in particular: go where your type of guy goes. If you want to find a certain type, you will have to go to the places where your type hangs out. This can be any number of places. Go back to the list of character traits you just made and take a long look at them. Where would guys with the character traits you want be found? Dances, bars, and hanging out at the local convenience store? Volunteering, church services and activities, college classes and clubs? Work, business get-togethers, sporting events, exercise clubs, grocery stores? No matter the answer to this question, that is where you may have to go to be around the type of man who will be your prince. One important thing to consider: Look at the traits you listed, and make sure you have them as well. You need to work on acquiring the positive traits so your "dream guy" will be attracted to you too.

IS HE A FROG OR A PRINCE?

hen you have thought about what kind of person you are looking for, consider whether the person meets those standards. If you have considered the way he treats people, and he still seems to measure up, move to the next step. What's the next step? It's to find at least three people who have known this potential prince for a long time and ask them what he's really like. Try to do this before you become too close to him or involved too deeply to think clearly. The following list can help you as you try to decide if the guy you are dating is a frog or a prince.

FROG INDICATORS

There are a lot of behaviors that people have. Some of them we understand. Some of them confuse us. Some are clearly froggy. Some are just idiosyncrasies. We can't go into depth about all the different possibilities here, but we do want to give you some idea of those behaviors that give strong indications that the guy you are interested in may indeed be a frog. Keep in mind that just because he might have one or two goofy tendencies, or wart behaviors, he still may not be a frog. However, if he has quite a few then you should seriously reconsider whether you want to keep dating him or move on. He may not be the guy for you and there are many other options. So don't feel like you have to overlook negative behaviors or signs just so you can have a guy in your life. Never settle. Always go for what's best for you.

The following signs could be considered warts. If a guy shows many of these warts, it's a pretty good indication he is a frog. The people you date and the person you marry can't be perfect of course, but you should at least feel happier when you are around them.

DOES HE HAVE WARTS?

Do the sentences below describe your date or your relationship?

- ♛ You often feel bad, depressed, or less like a complete person after you've been with him.

- ♛ Much of your time with him is spent "helping" him, fighting with him, worrying about not making him angry, or defending yourself verbally.

- ♛ All your friends and family say he's bad for you, but you find yourself insisting they don't really know him.

- ♛ You find yourself constantly disagreeing about important things in life, such as your values.

- ♛ He doesn't seem to listen to you or take an interest in what is important to you.

- ♛ You feel like his therapist.

- ♛ You enjoy the wild emotional swings of the relationship.

- ♛ He seems reluctant to talk about serious matters or to express his emotions to you, except to complain about his world or his family.

♛ You find that you know very little about him, even after spending a lot of time with him, and he seems reluctant to tell you about himself.

♛ You feel afraid to express your own opinions around him.

♛ He pressures you for more physical/sexual contact than you want.

♛ He doesn't do well with kids. They bother him or he teases even after they tell him to stop.

♛ He has been abused physically, sexually or verbally and, despite lots of warning signs (explosive anger, tendency to zone out emotionally) claims that it's not a problem and refuses to talk about it or see someone professionally about it.

♛ He is constantly blaming someone else for his problems.

♛ He is physically abusive to you (hits, slaps, kicks, restrains, or threatens to hurt you).

♛ You want to help him work through some problem in his life.

If you answered "yes" to any of the questions it is not a good sign. If you answered yes to several you should seriously look at not dating this guy and moving on to others. The more "yes's" you answered the more it should indicate that you should be thinking about running not just walking away from this guy. If he has been abusive in any way (calling you names, yelling at you, hitting or threatening you), no matter how much you think you love this guy you need to get out as fast as your legs can carry you. Don't look back. Don't wonder if you will miss him or regret leaving. You may experience all that but you will also feel worse if you don't. Don't let him persuade you to stay by him saying, "I'll stop." He won't. It might get better for a while, but that kind of behavior almost always gets worse with time. Life is too short to spend it with someone who treats you this way.

Keep in mind that there are a lot of frogs in the pond and you shouldn't have to settle for one that will stay that way all his life, or even part of his life if it is the part that you are in.

PRINCE INDICATORS

After reading about frogs and frog traits, you are probably wondering if there are any potential princes out there for you. There are, sometimes you just may not recognize them at first.

For instance, a group of women all had a mutual admiration for a male coworker because of his inner qualities. In talking about him, they agreed that he was the type of guy they should have dated but always thought was too nerdy in high school. He was always a prince but was only discovered when they changed their priorities of what was important in a man.

This is an example of several women who figured out later in life what really made up a prince. After several failed relationships and repeated attempts to find a good man, they had come to have a better understanding of what a real prince was like. You will have to go through the same process of discovery. Hopefully, you will figure it out earlier than these women. Before you are married is the time to get to know a lot of guys. Don't limit yourself. Take the time to get to know them. Really explore the way they treat people. Keep your eyes open, especially if you find yourself "swept off your feet." Pay attention and ask yourself the frog and the prince questions in this chapter. They will really help you sort through much of the confusion that comes with guys and relationships.

The following is a list of things to look for that likely indicate he is a prince:

Do the sentences below describe your date or your relationship?

- ♛ He is kind and attentive to you.

- ♛ He's easy to talk to.

- ♛ He listens to you.

- ♛ He shares his emotional world with you, but not in a way that asks you to help him work it out.

- ♛ His emotional world is stable, or at least there is stability in his life or family life.

- ♛ He wants to learn about your interests and his interests seem similar to yours.

- ♛ He deals with frustration responsibly. He tries to resolve the situation rather than approaching it with rage or violence.

- ♛ He is respectful and kind to people he doesn't have to be nice to or who can't help him "get ahead."

- ♛ He's kind to his family and to children.

♛ You find yourself caring more about yourself, your future, others and him because of your relationship with him.

♛ He values your opinion.

♛ He is respectful of your time and schedule and doesn't just call last minute for a date or activity.

♛ He is able to share his feelings and concerns about life and relationships.

♛ He builds you up, but not just to flatter you.

♛ He praises you and your good qualities, but not just to make up or try to get something from you.

♛ He cares about your goals and your future.

♛ He encourages you to have friends and to spend time with them as well as with him.

♛ He cares about his family even if he isn't getting along with them at the present time.

♛ He encourages you to do your best.

♛ You feel like being a better person when you are around him.

♛ He feels like your best friend.

♛ You feel that you can be yourself and don't have to act differently than you normally would just so you don't fear losing him.

♛ He's okay showing emotion.

♛ He remembers special occasions.

♛ He is very loyal to you and others in his life.

♛ He can stick with a project until it's finished.

♛ He doesn't give up when life challenges seem too much.

How many "yes"' answers did you have? If you answered "yes" to most or all then your guy might be prince material. Congratulations on a good find. You are fortunate. But remember, this is just a general questionnaire to get you to take a look at your guy and to help you weed out the frogs.

If, on the other hand, you answered "no" to several it can be a sign that he might not be your prince. It might be a sign that he might in fact be a frog. Be honest with yourself. These questions are meant to help you. If your guy didn't score quite as well as you hoped, take it at face value. Let it be a warning sign to you. Either you don't know him well enough or you do and he doesn't add up to prince material. Either way, it is not a very good sign if he only scored a few "yes's".

MATURITY IS A GOOD THING

ou will probably discover as you go through the dating adventure that there are many frogs and very few princes. But, as we have pointed out before, most guys will turn out to be somebody's Prince. And some guys that seem like frogs can make amazing transformations into princes later in life. This is what happens to frogs in life. A frog starts out as an egg. It hatches as a tadpole and looks nothing like a frog. After a while the tadpole starts to change. It grows hind legs, then front legs. The head begins to change and the tail begins to shrink and soon disappears completely as the frog matures into an adult.

The change process is known as metamorphosis, or the changing from one form to another. Nowadays, it is often referred to as "morphing." A major reason you should date a lot of different guys is to find out which characteristics you like. The major reason you are reading this book is to find out what type of guys to avoid who are frogs and who will never morph into a prince. Through this process you should be more likely to be able to identify those guys who may seem like frogs now but are likely to morph into princes.

Some boys who are definitely teenage frogs become adult princes. Often this is because the boy changes and matures. Sometimes it is because the girl's perspective changes as she matures. We've talked a lot about personality and perspective in Chapter 2. Both are important in the great metamorphosis. What you look for in a mate changes as you age. For example, at age 25, dating the captain of the high school football team is probably no longer important. You may decide that communication is what is important to you, and you will discount the guys that were "challenging" in high school because they kept you playing the "Does he like me, or doesn't he?" guessing game. Different guys become attractive to you for different reasons as you mature.

Remember that princes are out there, but they just may look like frogs. That is, they may seem, at first, uninteresting or boring. And remember also, that it may take a while to find out what they're really like.

Here's "The Great Secret" — it's how they treat you, others, and themselves that make these men princes. You may have to work somewhat harder and expend more effort to discover that.

PLAYING HARD-TO-GET

here are times when you'll probably wonder if the guy you're interested in is trying to play hard-to-get. Playing hard-to-get can come from several places.

♚ He may be insecure or unsure about how you feel about him so he will seem distant as a means of protecting his pride. Remember what was mentioned earlier about guys and losing? If he is unsure about how interested you are in him, he may be hiding his feelings. It might seem childish to you, but it is probably very important to him.

♚ He may really like you, but he may be afraid of letting his buddies in on it for fear of them giving him a hard time. He keeps his distance in front of his friends, but later gives you a call. This can be confusing to you, but give it some consideration.

♚ He may not be interested. His behavior may in fact be telling you that he has no further interest. Be careful not to interpret this as playing hard-to-get. You will be setting yourself up for a big let down.

So with all these mixed signals how do you know if he likes you? That is the question of the ages. It can sometimes be very difficult. You can do some of the things we talked about in the flirting section of this chapter. Flirting behaviors can test the water to see how he responds to you. You can wait to see if he calls or if he shows some interest. You can also take the direct approach and show him your interest, or even ask him out. If he says 'no' then you have your answer.

When you like someone it will serve you well to keep in mind the things we talked about in the 'Why Do Guys Act Like They Do' section. Guys are competitive and they like to compete. They like the thrill of the chase. When women are too accessible, too easy to catch, they often lose interest and move on. So if you like some guy and seem too available to him, he may not be as interested so you may want to do a little playing hard-to-get of your own.

It's a basic tendency for human beings to fail to treasure what they did not have to work for, and guys are particularly notorious for this. For instance, we appreciate our health most when we are recovering from an illness. Also, the satisfaction of obtaining a good grade is almost always greater if we had to work hard to get it. In the same way, a guy will generally be more interested in someone who seems a little bit unobtainable. If you find that you are the one who is always making the phone calls, or approaching him in the hall, or trying to find out where he is going to be so you can try to see him, then you are perhaps putting too much into establishing a relationship. You may want to hold back a little to see if he picks up the relationship slack.

This is not playing mind games. You are simply establishing the fact that you respect yourself, and that his interest in you must be equal to yours in him or you will, after giving him a reasonable chance to respond, be moving on in your quest to find a prince. If he doesn't respond to you then move on. Remember the "many frogs in the pond" concept. Keep looking.

BUILD YOURSELF

 f you are having trouble finding someone to date, you are not being asked out much, or you have been rejected, we recommend that you go to work on the most important thing you will ever do— becoming the person you want to become.

Most people in the early stage of dating try to put their "best foot forward." You don't want to make a negative first, second or third impression. We all have positive and negative character traits and some of them are not obvious to us. These are what we call personality "blind spots." Other people, however, can see these traits clearly. We covered this in the second chapter of the book. If you find that people you date generally have the same reaction to you, and that reaction is negative, it is important to ask yourself whether these people have identified a blind spots.

Here are some questions you should ask yourself:

- 👑 Am I having trouble attracting people I want to date because of something about me?

- 👑 If so, can I identify what these personal issues might be?

- 👑 If I can identify these issues, are they things I can change (for example, be more friendly, talk less about myself, work on being less introverted, getting professional help if need be and so forth)?

♕ If they are things I can change (and here's the most important question) do I want to change myself in these ways? Is it worth changing a part of me to be something that potential dates might want?

The most interesting potential partners are those who have worked to create an attractive personality by taking advantage of their strengths and overcoming their weaknesses.

To make any relationship work, we must all adjust and change somewhat. Yet some people would rather be true to themselves regardless of whether that repels other people. Again, this choice is entirely up to you. Remember also that the people who have found these character traits to be unattractive are not the final judge of what is acceptable—you may find someone wonderful who is attracted to you for the very reasons others were turned off.

But, if you decide that you want to change yourself to become more attractive to guys, we recommend working through the following process:

1. Determine that you want to change mainly for you and not because you think some guy will like you better if you do.

2. Decide what kind of guys you really want to date.

3. Try to determine what kind of girls guys of this type would likely be attracted to.

4. Decide if these traits are positive enough that if you developed them, you would feel like a better person. Sometimes we look at a particular group and decide we want to become like them, only to discover that they are generally unhappy. (Like people that make fun of others thinking it is cool, or kids that act snobby and exclude others.) However, if you decide that these traits are what you desire, go on to the next step.

5. Work to improve yourself according to what you want to be like. The key word here is "improve." This means if you are going to change you should change for the better. Take on positive traits and avoid negative traits that may seem acceptable just in order to fit in.

If you want to date a certain type of prince, become the type of princess you would want to date. If you want a prince, you must come to believe yourself equal to a prince. But it's not worth trying to become a person you don't like in order to please someone else. And we would also caution you to remember that even if you have worked for years to become a person who is attractive to what you think is a prince, you must still be willing to walk away from the relationship if you realize he is treating you like a frog would. You must be willing to say, "No matter how much I like you and want to be with you, if you do not treat me well, I am OK without you. I can make it on my own."

SEIZE THE DAY, SEIZE YOUR LIFE

If you are working to improve yourself, keep this sobering fact in mind: even though your self-improvement work may pay off, and you may be amazed at the difference in you, there is still no guarantee you will find what you are looking for. This is one of the most difficult things we must write about. Because there is no guarantee that you will find your prince, we recommend that you do one thing in particular: don't wait for your prince. Go for your life. Jump into the things you love. Do the things you want without waiting around. Be the person you want to be and, if you find your prince, so much the better. If you do this and you do find your prince, you will most likely find a better prince because you will be a better person and expect more for yourself. Work on yourself. You will never regret it.

It is infinitely easier to make a relationship work with another person if you are able to be a healthy person on your own. Two emotionally healthy people are much more able to withstand the hardships of close relationships than those who are desperate to have someone to lean on.

WHY DO I KEEP DATING THE SAME TYPE OF GUY?

 fter you have looked at the traits you have and analyzed the guys you have dated, try to find a theme. Do you seem to date the same type of guy over and over even though they always seem to treat you the same way (badly) and you came away feeling the same way (vowing never to date a guy like that again)? Many girls find themselves attracted to certain guys even though they recognize that these guys are not good for them. If that is the case, it's time to re-examine what might be happening in your mind as you are looking for your prince.

If you find that you tend to date the same type of guy again and again, and he always turns out to make you feel less valuable and less capable, reevaluate what it is about these guys that interests you. If you are tired of relationships that always seem to make you feel poorly about yourself or keep you on an emotional rollercoaster, maybe you are ready to start your search for a really good guy.

AM I ACTUALLY ATTRACTED TO FROGS?

Many girls worry they will never find the right guy, that is, a "nice" guy, who will treat them well without playing mind games. But when we talk to them as therapists about the type they say they are interested in, they often admit they have met nice guys before and have chosen not to pursue these relationships. This happens for many reasons:

NOT EXCITING ENOUGH

One young woman, Ann, recounted that "nice guys" often ask her out but that she makes excuses not to go out with them. She says that after she turns them away she feels very frustrated with herself. "There was this great guy I'd had my eye on for a while," she said, "and when he finally began to act interested, I began to give him the cold shoulder. Then I realized that, for some reason, I found him less exciting than other guys."

One of the most common reasons why girls never find the prince is that they find themselves attracted to the "bad-boy" types—that is, they are attracted to the frogs. What's the attraction? These men live "on the edge." They may drive fast, use drugs, fight often, and can be difficult to reach emotionally or play hard to get. If you crave excitement in your life, these men may look interesting and strong. They promise excitement and they deliver on that promise. These relationships may also cause a sensation among friends and family which can provide the attention some girls may crave, even if this attention is negative. These guys are a challenge for girls. Girls think, on an unconscious level, that if they can get a guy that is this difficult then they have won a great battle. To some girls, creating a relationship with a seemingly impossible guy is similar to a guy making an incredible catch on the football field. The challenge and the near impossibility of each brings amazement and envy from others, and a sense of personal accomplishment from oneself.

Another reason bad boys may be attractive to these girls is the sense of strength they display. As we discussed earlier, many girls look to someone physically or socially powerful as a protector (a knight in shining armor coming to take you away to live happily ever after) and to take care of them. These girls may believe that "nice guys" lack the strength to provide for them. Just the opposite is usually the case in today's relationships. The bad-boys often end up being neglectful and abusive in the relationship. The nice guys often turn out to be the best providers and best companions.

While it may be thrilling and interesting to flirt with bad boys, be sure to ask yourself whether this type of person is one you would be interested in spending your life with. How interesting will he be when the novelty of his "dangerous" behavior wears off? (And believe it, it will wear off! It always does.) Is he responsible? Will he be around physically and emotionally for you? For his children? We discuss more about some of these men and those like them in Chapter 8.

I WANT TO HELP HIM

Some girls date guys they know have serious problems because they want to rescue them. These girls may believe that if they "give of themselves" enough, these guys will change and "reach their potential," this is called "care-taking" in relationships. While there are instances of girls being able to somehow work a change in guys like this, quite the opposite usually happens. The guy usually pulls the girl into an endless series of discussions and late night chats, none of which ever really solve the problem. It is very difficult, if not impossible, to be a girlfriend and therapist at the same time. It's a big job to be a therapist and not one that is recommended for most people. Far from helping them, these discussions may even cause men to prolong their problems in order to be with their "therapist" more often. They get your attention because of their problems. If the problems go away, then so will the attention you are giving him. Therefore, he can't get better because he will lose you. It is a vicious cycle

Care-taking girls usually have great difficulty saying 'no'. You really want to help. You get a sense of value from it. But, if it continues, you will become emotionally drained. Usually, neither is he saved nor do you become the savior. It becomes tiring and frustrating to both of you and you usually end up resenting each other because neither one of you can live up to the expectations you began the relationship with.

I DON'T DESERVE HIM

Some girls feel quite the opposite of trying to heal or help. They may meet a good guy and immediately feel a sense of unworthiness when they are around him. They feel that he could be with someone "better" than they are. These girls almost always feel that they are somehow inferior and that they don't deserve the best. While this feeling is often complex, it can often be traced to their relationships with parents, especially fathers. It is very common for girls to look for men who remind them of their father, the man they are most, or wish to be the most, familiar with. If the fathers of these girls were abusive, chauvinistic, distant, rejecting, or abandoned them (such as by divorce or even death), their daughters tend to seek men who are similar to their fathers. Girls who have experienced abandonment or abuse or rejection tend to believe that it is their fault, that if they weren't so bad they wouldn't be rejected by the man that is supposed to love them the most, their father. When they get into a relationship or meet a guy that actually treats them with respect and care they feel that they don't deserve this good of a guy. They are either not that attracted to the "good" guy, or they say, "He doesn't really turn me on," or they find some way to sabotage the relationship so he stops calling or breaks it off. All the while wishing for exactly the kind of guy they are pushing away.

I DON'T WANT TO BE ALONE

Many girls date guys because they don't want to be alone. Some girls think being alone means that they are a failure. They believe being alone, especially on a weekend night, means that nobody wants them. Girls that think this way are setting themselves up to be with almost any guy. They think, "If I don't date him, I might be alone," something that for them is a terrible thing. More often than not, the guys they end up with are not only frogs, worse yet, they may even be predators. These girls haven't discovered what you learned in Chapter 2: that if a girl is comfortable with who she is when she is alone, she is much more likely to be happy when trying to make relationships work. If you feel this way, ask yourself, "Do I feel comfortable being with myself?" If the answer is 'no' then you are setting yourself up to look for a guy to fill your loneliness. If this feels like you, then go back to Chapter 2 and work on yourself with the help of some of the quizzes and exercises. Work on you. You are worth it. Go for it.

I WANT A STRONG GUY TO BE WITH

Many women fall into the "the strong guy is better" mode of thinking. They believe, on some level, these guys will give them a sense of protection and identity. It's natural to want to be protected and cared for. But someone else shouldn't give you a sense of identity. Some girls lack a well-defined sense of self and hope to find this through the men they date. They think that the "strong, silent" type is very desirable.

Strong-acting guys are not necessarily the most likely to be good providers or protectors. They probably won't even be good boyfriends. They tend to be impenetrable, emotionally distant and often insecure. You may never see this because they are so busy putting up a strong front. Granted, this is a generalization, but if you find that you are attracted to the strong, silent types that seem powerful, make sure that he comes from a good family and that his personality is just shy and not emotionally distant. How do you find that out? Check it out with his friends, with his neighbors, with his past girl-friends. This may seem like a lot of work, but it could save you a lot of pain.

The strong acting guys are not necessarily the most likely to be successful in the world of work either. If they turn out to be aggressive (which is often the case), using their strength to get their way, they tend to be prone to using violence both inside and outside the home. Research on aggressive and violent men shows that this style of interacting is much more likely to offend people with whom they do business. Their sense of who they are comes from being stronger than others, usually physically, and sometime verbally. When they become adults, their physical strength no longer means they are strong in areas of business. They usually don't make very good companions, because they will likely treat you the same way.

I HAVEN'T LEARNED TO SAY 'NO'

Learning to say "no" to a guy is an important part of taking care of yourself. If you find it difficult to say "no" to a guy, that says something about you. What it might be saying is that you don't want to hurt his feelings. If this is the reason, it is better to tell him "no" up front than to string him along. It also might be saying you are afraid of what he might do or how he might act if you say no. In this case, he has probably given you some indication that he is aggressive and perhaps even dangerous. Aggressive guys scare girls with their harsh personalities. Typically, this aggression doesn't show up until you are too deep into the relationship to get out easily. At first, these guys are all compliments and chocolates. It isn't until later that the anger rears its ugly head. Girls then often find themselves in a relationship they don't want, but are afraid to leave. Some guys (and girls too) who are aggressive can be dangerous, especially when you try to break up. That is why you need to learn to avoid these guys before getting involved romantically. Not starting a relationship with them is the best way to not have to be afraid of them. Stand up for yourself in the beginning of the relationship.

If you find yourself in a relationship with a guy who scares you, you should immediately get out. The longer you stay the harder it will be to leave. Don't fool yourself by thinking, "He has good qualities too," or "If I just love him enough he will change." It usually doesn't work that way. Don't think you are going to be the magician that changes him. That is a dangerous fantasy.

The most important thing for you to do is to let other people know about your fears, get them to support your decision to leave the relationship and, if you need it, get them to help you end the relationship. Your parents are the best ones to help you do this. If your parents won't or can't help, then you can get help from other people, and even the law if it comes to that. Take the necessary steps to end the relationship now. It will be better in the long run. You will have learned who not to get involved with, how to identify aggressive behavior, and how to get out of a bad relationship.

SAYING 'NO' TO A DATE

here will come a time when some guy will ask you out. You may or may not want to go out with him. If you don't want to go out with him, you have to tell him "no". If you do go out with him and you continue dating him, there will probably come a time when you don't want to go out anymore. In either case, you are going to have to tell him. Likewise, the same may happen to you.

Guys and girls see rejection differently. As we discussed earlier, to both guys and girls, rejection often means he or she loses, so they may see themselves as less of a man or woman. But girls and guys like to have the rejection served up differently. In most cases, it is better to tell a guy straight out that you don't want to date him. Women, on the other hand, typically like to be let down easy. In the event you have to do the rejecting, keep this in mind. Don't let a guy down easy as you would have him do you. In other words, don't give hints, or act like you still want to have a relationship by stringing them along. The guy will not get the message. He will keep calling you if he sees any hope of dating you. You may try to let him down easy when he asks you out by saying something like, "I can't tonight or this weekend." You then avoid him at school or around town thinking he will get the hint. But he doesn't. He takes you at your word and calls again and asks you out. You may even put him off again, but you may also agree to go out with him because you don't want to hurt him. This may go on for some time until you finally just come out and tell him you don't want to go out anymore. Indeed he will be hurt, but if you would have told him "no" earlier, he would be over it by now.

If he does the rejecting, you can expect him to be more straightforward and perhaps just tell you straight out. This may hurt you a lot because you would prefer to be let down easy. But that's not how guys do it, so it may seem unusually cruel to you. Don't take it so hard. It does hurt, but it's just a difference between guys and girls.

If you get rejected, it will hurt, even if it's only a little. Chances are it will hurt a lot. There are some things you can do to make the pain less or not last as long. The most important things you can do are:

👑 Keep in mind that his rejection does not mean you are any less valuable.

♛ Take it for what it is: simply someone (not your prince) growing tired of a relationship. It's probably the best thing because you can move on in your life.

♛ Keep yourself busy with projects and friends. Friends are the best remedy to get over being rejected. Remember Princess Kate? When she was completely devastated by the frogspell, who did she run to? Her best friend, Mary. And Mary ran to Kate when she was down. They helped each other through the bad times and enjoyed the good times together.

♛ Find somebody else to be interested in. Don't grab the first guy that notices you or that catches your eye. Be discriminating and keep your self-respect. But it's OK to start looking for the next guy to get to know. That's the dating cycle.

SEXUAL AND PHYSICAL ATTRACTION

eing physically attracted to your dates is natural and expected. That strong attraction is sometimes hard to fight against. Almost everybody who has been around the dating scene for any amount of time has had this feeling. It is an infatuation and can even seem overwhelming and out of your control. Sexual attraction, while important, is not the foundation of a good relationship. In fact, if that is the main attraction, it will usually dominate the relationship and become the only thing that keeps you together. This doesn't let you grow personally. It doesn't let the relationship grow. It can lead to feelings of being used for your body. And it creates a shallow relationship that can be broken with the slightest difficulty or at the temptation of another person.

If sexual attraction is the basis for your relationship, the guy you are dating may also be pressuring you for more sexual contact than you feel comfortable with. Sex and intimacy are wonderful and will complement a fulfilling relationship, but they are only part of the relationship. You will never regret waiting until you are married to have sex, but you will almost surely regret not waiting.

Sex is a moral, as well as a spiritual issue. Sex outside of marriage affects your moral strength. It also negatively affects your personal spirituality. Beyond moral reasons, here are some others to think about and to say to him in response to the pressure:

♛ You are setting yourself up for a bad reputation. Do you want to be known as "easy"? Do you want guys pursuing you for the wrong reasons?

♛ There is always the risk for sexually transmitted diseases, even with properly used forms of birth control. This is a real and serious reality. When you have sex with someone, you run the risk of getting any sexual transmitted diseases of his previous sexual partners.

♛ Sexual contact leads to deeper and often more confusing emotions and boundary problems with that person and with others you will date in the future.

♛ Much research and a tremendous amount of clinical experience tells one thing about premarital sexual relations—it will NOT help your relationship. In fact, it almost always makes the relationship worse. If the relationship is not good, it will create more things to argue about.

♛ Having sex, becoming more experienced, will not help your future relationships if the present one doesn't work out. Sex is something you work on with your partner and it usually takes some time to get good with each other. Sexual experience will not ensure a good relationship in the future.

♛ Once you start, it is extremely difficult to stop the next time. It becomes much more difficult to not keep going "there" after you have engaged in sexual contact.

♛ It creates confusing dynamics in the relationship, like thinking that, "If you love me, you will have sex with me." Sex does not equal love.

♛ When you do get married, there will be the tendency to compare your spouse with previous sexual partners and that could cause some problems in your marriage. You may think that you would be more experienced and could give your spouse better, more fulfilling sex, but that is a false belief.

♛ If you do wait until you are married to have sex, you will never have to worry about comparing or being compared with other lovers. Research about that very subject indicates that those who wait until after marriage to have sex are more intimate with feelings and with their bodies. They are typically more secure with their relationships and find the relationships more stable and fulfilling overall.

Remember also: if the guy you are dating keeps pressuring you for sexual contact beyond what you feel comfortable doing, this is a sure sign that he is not a prince. An even more sure sign that a guy is a predator is if he tells you that, "If you really love me, you will have sex with me." Sex includes oral and other sexual touching and not just intercourse. You never have to have sex in order to "keep" a true prince. Don't let him convince you otherwise. If he keeps trying after you have said "no," that is a sure sign he is a predator. Don't put up with it. Leave him in the swamp and go after your prince.

HELP FOR PARENTS

Parents frequently ask themselves what they can do to help their daughters choose their dates wisely. Here are a few suggestions:

♕ Let your kids know you love them in a way they can accept. Give them limits without screaming, or excessive punishment. You are the parent. It is your job to set limits. It's not always a very pleasant part of the job but you've got to do it. The earlier in their life you start, the better off you'll be later.

♕ Set calm (reasonable and well thought out, not spur of the moment) limits throughout their lives (especially when they are young) so they understand that you set limits in order to protect them, not to annoy or punish them when they are dating. They will also be more capable of setting their own limits and sticking to them.

♕ Don't encourage them to have dating relationships early on in their lives. Some mothers talk about dating, sex and boys with their 10-year-old daughters as if they were 16 or 17-year-old girls. Talk to them about sex when they begin to notice differences. Each child will be open to the discussion of sex at a different age, but you should always talk about sex in an age appropriate manner, and only discuss as much as you need to. Don't discuss it in a way that encourages them to get involved at a young age. They need your help to be protected against the onslaught of life they are facing.

♕ Have talks with them periodically throughout their lives to help them understand that there is an appropriate dating age and that they shouldn't try to push premature opposite sex relationships.

♕ Throughout their childhood, establish and maintain good relationships with your kids. Spend time with them. Give of yourself. Be available emotionally. Try to establish relationships of trust and communication during the years so that when they have questions about the person they are dating, they will come to you.

♕ When they talk, listen. Try to make yourself available to them when they want to talk. Don't always be ready with a word of advice or counsel. Most of the time they don't want advice, even if they ask for it. They just want to talk and tell you what is on their mind. If you allow them to come to you with the small things and just listen with out advising, which can be difficult at times, they will be more likely to come to you with the big things. They will also be more likely to come to you when they do want advice. But what you will find is that many times they will know what to do with their life dilemmas without your advice. They just need to vent.

♛ Teach your daughter she always has the right to say "no" to unwanted attention or affection. And let her know that you will back her up 100%. She needs to know you support her. Knowing this gives her needed strength to stand up for herself.

♛ Be a good example. If you are married, be in love with your spouse. Tell each other of your love. Do things daily that show your love. The best way to help your children in their relationships is to show them how good relationships are done. Show them a good marital relationship so they will not seek out guys, and especially frogboys, to fill the void they feel in their lives. This will help them become whole people.

♛ Get education about parenting skills, and relationship skills. A very small percentage of people actually have the skills necessary to have great relationships and to be great parents without additional information. And even those who do could get even better by learning other skills and gaining knowledge. Always be open to learning, especially about being a parent and having good relationships.

♛ Try to involve yourself in the dating lives of your children. Meet the guys she dates. Ask them to come into the house. Talk to them. Ask them about their lives, interests, etc. And remember to let them know that THEY ARE TAKING OUT YOUR MOST PRECIOUS POSSESSION. Give them your rules: When should they have her home, how you expect her to be treated, etc. They need to understand your concern and what you will tolerate and what you will not tolerate. After the date, ask your daughter how her date went. Discuss it with her.

♛ Take interest in your daughter's life. Never be too busy to spend time with her and for her. Attend her school, civic and church functions. Know what she is doing and what she is involved in, both good and bad. Encourage her to strive for excellence and goals.

♛ Be a parent first and a friend second. There is a trend of parents wanting to be "best friends" with their children. They think that being a peer will make their job as parents more manageable. It actually is a way of avoiding the responsibility of being a parent. Being a parent is not always easy. Sometimes you must put your foot down and say "no." A peer can't do that as a parent must. When your daughter becomes an adult, you will become best friends if you treat her with love and respect. When she is a teenager and young adult, she needs your love, wisdom and guidance, not your friendship.

♛ What about if you started dating before you were 16? Dating these days can be more problematic than when you were teenagers. There is greater acceptance of sexual experimentation, greater likelihood of sexual involvement, and greater risk of contracting deadly sexually transmitted diseases. Earlier in the book, we talked about other reasons to wait until at least age 16 to date.

♛ Understand that no matter how much she seems to be trying to push you away or how angry she is at you, deep down she still wants you and needs you. This is probably the most frustrating aspect of parenting. It is also the most frustrating thing for your daughter. The crazy emotions and internal struggle to find herself, (to separate and become an individual) yet stay connected with you and the family tears her apart emotionally too. She is usually too overwhelmed to know how to deal with it. Think back on your adolescent years and you will probably remember going through a similar struggle. You must be the rock of her foundation. You must keep the home hearth warm and inviting so that eventually, on her terms, she can return to your home and know that she is loved.

CHAPTER 5

HAVE I FOUND A PRINCE

ou've been wading through the murky bog of dating. You've encountered various frogs. You've dated some with potential. You've dated some that will definitely be frogs forever. Regardless of where you are at in your dating career, you should always be looking to date potential princes. They may not be Your Prince, but princes just the same. This chapter helps you look a little closer at the guys you are interested in.

Until you are about 20 or 21, the ideal dating situation is to not tie yourself to one guy. This will give you the opportunity to have fun getting to know a variety of personality types, doing fun activities, and practicing communicating and interacting with the opposite sex. Even if you are dating one guy more steadily than others, dating others keeps you in the mix and allows you to continue having fun with a variety of guys.

Having "fun" in the dating process means you are not always thinking, "Is he the one?" If you are constantly thinking about this it puts an enormous amount of pressure on you and your date. Dating for fun means you care more about getting to know your date and his characteristics, than trying to figure out "Is this going to work?"

When you date for fun you'll be more willing to date a wider variety of guys because you won't feel the need to eliminate ones that don't immediately appear to meet your criteria for the man of your dreams. When you continue to date a wide variety of guys you'll get an even better sense of what kind of guy will really be your prince. You'll become more discerning, seeing through the frog exterior that many guys put on to make them seem attractive. In addition, if you get into a relationship that is not good or that turns bad after a while, you'll be able to get out faster and with minimal emotional damage.

If you have dated wisely in your teens, and you continue to date a variety of guys, you will have a better idea of what you are looking for in Your Prince. As you enter young adulthood you can better identify those guys who you want to spend more time with and those you want to avoid. As you begin to get more serious you won't have to put up with as many frogs.

DATING FOR SERIOUS

ating for serious (looking for Your Prince) should come at a time in your life when you have matured emotionally, and psychologically. It should come after you have dated a lot of different types of guys with different personalities, likes and interests so you have a pretty clear idea of what you like and don't like in a guy. It should come at a point in your life when you find yourself ready to be more serious about one guy than other guys.

You might be asking yourself, "Just how do I know if I am ready?" In an earlier chapter we discussed the idea that you marry who you date. This concept is especially true if you date seriously or go steady. If you are dating seriously before you are emotionally and developmentally ready you are increasing the odds of getting too involved, getting pregnant, or even deciding to get married at too young an age. Research, logic, and experience indicates that the earliest most people are ready emotionally and developmentally to get married is in the early twenties. It's interesting to note that the odds of marital success, meaning not getting divorced, stay fairly constant for couples who marry after about 23-years-old and older. The odds of divorce are very high for those who marry before 19. There are many possible reasons for this, but we believe a major reason is that from the ages of 19 to about 21 people go through a developmental change from adolescents into young adulthood. It is a critical time in the developmental process that all of us go through. A person who marries before making this developmental transition takes on the responsibilities of adults before she or he is actually ready. Often, many people that marry before age 20 later in life begin to feel they haven't "lived" or experienced life. They often feel they have missed out on something and become dissatisfied with their marriage with life.

₍now that many teenagers have their first "boyfriend" experience long ₋e they are ready for a long-term committed relationship. Even at a ₋ng age, if you have a boyfriend he should still be a good candidate for a ₋g-term committed relationship if you were older. If you choose to go ₋eady you should keep this book at your side and pay attention to how you feel when you are with him and how he treats you. Don't hesitate to get out of the relationship if things are not good. Don't be like Princess Kate and stay with him when he does things that indicate his "frogginess" just to make sure you have a boyfriend. Remember we talked about being with a guy just because you are afraid of being alone. This is a bad sign at any time in your dating life. It is even more dangerous when you are getting more serious about finding your prince.

CONVENIENCE DATING

lyss was one of those girls who didn't think she was all that pretty. She would look at herself in the mirror and see bulges and bumps and think that if only she could get rid of those she might be acceptable. She used to spend nights dreaming about dating, but at the same time she was afraid. She thought if she had a boyfriend that sooner or later he would see her faults and not be interested in her anymore. She saw so many girls hanging out with their boyfriends and wished she had someone who would pay that kind of attention to her.

There was one guy, Kevin, who seemed to be interested in her. He wasn't what she was looking for in many ways, so at first she said "no" when he asked her out. But Kevin kept calling, and instead of sitting at home alone when all her friends were out on dates, she finally accepted his invitation. They went out several times. He kept calling. She kept accepting dates with him. Eventually she didn't accept dates from other guys just because she knew Kevin would call and she didn't want to disappoint him by telling him that she was busy. They ended up going to all the school dances and events together. When her friends asked her if they were going steady, she would say they weren't. But she just kept going out with him because she could count on him to ask her out, and she decided it wasn't all that bad being with him.

Like Elyss and Kevin, some relationships "happen" either because the participants are bored, are too insecure to pursue someone else, or because no one else seems interested. This is not steady dating but "convenience dating." Convenience dating can become a problem if you continue to date without feeling anything "special" in the relationship. These relationships can progress until partners have spent so much time together that several situations may develop:

- ♛ The relationship can become so convenient that both partners choose each other through default, even though he or she might not really feel like they want spend years of their lives with this person. Many dismal marriages have been the result of relationships becoming too convenient. You start to think that dating this person is better than being alone.

- ♛ Outsiders who may want to date either of the partners may look at them and believe they are a couple. This prevents them from being asked out by other people who may be more compatible.

- ♛ The more time spent together, the more likely it is that partners will become sexually involved, with the resulting risk of emotional confusion, sexually transmitted diseases and pregnancy.

- ♛ People who marry out of convenience almost always look back with regrets about not dating someone else.

Don't date out of convenience or fear of being alone! If he keeps asking you, don't accept dates out of habit. It is far better to risk hurting someone by saying "no" in the short term than to forge a relationship with someone you know in your heart or head is not right for you. And remember this: It is never too late to get out a bad relationship—even if you are walking down the aisle at your wedding ceremony. There are too many people—girls and guys—who knew in their hearts that it was wrong to marry that particular person even while they were saying, "I do."

PRACTICING WHILE YOU DATE

art of a healthy relationship is discovering activities you enjoy together. This should be one of the most fun parts of the dating process. So, make sure you are not doing the same old thing every time you get together. Especially if that same old thing ends up being some level of sexual interaction. If all you have together is sex, or sexual play, that is a red flag for this relationship. Long-lasting relationships need more than sex to survive.

Try out some of the things on the list mentioned in Chapter 4 under Recommended Dating Activities. This is a great time of discovery. If you try various things together, you will have the opportunity to see how he reacts in a variety of situations. And he will have the same opportunity of getting to know you.

Tim and Ann were seniors in high school and had been going steady for six months. Ann read the FrogBuster and realized that most of her interaction with Tim was sexually charged. She decided to try out some of the recommended activities for dating and soon discovered that while Tim was a great "lover," he was actually a pretty boring guy. He didn't like the outdoors, didn't have a lot of plans for his future, and certainly wouldn't help Ann end up where she wanted to be in her life. She ended the relationship and started looking at the guys she dated in a different light so she could find her prince charming that could help make her dreams (the realistic ones) come true.

PRACTICING EFFECTIVE COMMUNICATION

The number one complaint of couples in therapy is that they don't communicate well. What this usually means is that when they disagree or argue, they stop communicating in a civil, respectful way and either clam up and walk away or say hurtful things. Conversations are hampered because of this repetitive cycle. The best time to figure out how to communicate effectively is while you are single, dating and engaged without the added stressors of marriage.

Engage your dates in conversations about subjects that are important to you such as what you think about life, your future, your family, and the family you want to have. Ask him how his family handles emotionally charged subjects. Does he say one or two things about it and try to change the subject? Or does he stay with the topic and share his point of view and feelings? Does he talk about things that are interesting only to him and avoid other subjects that might be interesting to you? If he talks only about himself or his interests, he may not be quite what you are looking for. Wouldn't you rather have someone to SHARE your world with and who wants to share his world with you? Work on understanding who he is and where he is coming from. See if he has any interest or desire to do the same for you.

In this chapter, we will look at various styles of communication. Keep in mind that people act differently in different situations, but if your dating a guy who exhibits many of the traits described in the first three columns in the following Styles of Communicating and Interacting Chart, you may want to stop dating him. This is especially true if you have identified traits in columns 2 and 3 more than two or three times or see one trait consistently over the course of your relationship.

STYLES OF COMMUNICATING AND INTERACTING CHART

Possible Frog	Most Likely a Frog	Possible Predator	Probable Prince
Self-pitying	Grudge carrying	Insisting	Clear about responsibility
Victim	Resentful	Dominating	Direct about feelings/thoughts
Overly apologetic	Spiteful/never apologizes	Pushy	Aware/appropriately apologetic
Self-punishing	Dishonest	Rude	Spontaneous
"Doormat"	Bitter	Overbearing	Energetic
Injured	Gossipy	Domineering	Powerful but not threatening
Avoiding	Malicious	Overpowering	Self motivated
Giving in	Revengeful	Violent	Real, without being forceful
Withdrawn	Unaware	Loud	Honest
Unresponsive	Manipulative	Destructive	Responsible for self
Sacrificing	Double messages	Hostile	Open
Always gives in	Indignant	Superior	Chooses positive responses
Inhibited	Cynical	Bossy	Behaves appropriately
Unexpressive	Two-faced	Mean	Negotiates when disagrees
No eye contact	Indirect	Thoughtless	Listens intently
Retreating	Phony	Threatening	Confident
Ignoring	Confusing	Explosive	Centered
Too Sweet	Confused	Always Right	Expresses himself without threats
Crying	Sarcastic	Ridiculing	Coping
Helpless	Sulky	Contemptuous/rigid	Flexible
Anxious	Pouting	Belittling	Confronts inequities
Humiliated	Uneasy	Inconsiderate	Vital/loves life
Insecure	Fearful	Preachy	In control of self
Self-denying	Anxious	Harsh	Considerate of self and others
Martyr	Insulted	Punishing	Competent
Timid	Devious	Invading	Relaxed
Takes abuse	Condescending	Interrupting	Respectful

Using the descriptive words and phrases from the Styles of Communicating and Interacting Chart on Page 125, how would you answer the following questions:

COMMUNICATION QUIZ

♛ When you get into an argument with your steady dating partner, how would you describe his actions?
Word(s)_____ Column _____

♛ When you get into a conversation that is interesting to you, but not to your partner, how does he respond?
Word(s)_____ Column _____

♛ When you talk about your plans for the future, how does he respond?
Word(s)_____ Column _____

♛ How is your boyfriend with children?

Word(s)_____ Column _____

♛ How is your boyfriend with people that annoy him?
Word(s)_____ Column _____

♛ How does he treat you generally?
Word(s)_____ Column _____

♛ How does he respond to stress and frustration?
Word(s)_____ Column _____

♛ How is he around new people and new situations?
Word(s)_____ Column _____

♛ How would you describe him to a friend?
Word(s)_____ Column _____

♛ How does he treat his mother or father?
Word(s)_____ Column _____

How many descriptive words did you indicate above from each column in the chart? Were any from the first three columns? If they were you should take a serious look at discontinuing your relationship with this guy. He is not going to be your prince and he may not be anybody's prince.

TAKING RESPONSIBILITY

Responsibility is another important thing in a healthy relationship. This stage in your dating is a good time to start paying attention to this. Taking responsibility for yourself is one of the foundations of a healthy life, and all healthy relationships. Many people go through life blaming everyone and everything for how their life has turned out. They seem to think that as long as somebody else or circumstances are at fault, then they don't have to be. Therefore, they can't be blamed for their life, their behavior, their thoughts, their failures, or their weaknesses. If the guy you are dating does not take personal responsibility for his life, it is a bad sign. A true prince takes responsibility for himself. He is proactive, takes charge of his life, and expects the same from those with whom he associates (including you). To help assess his level of personal responsibility use the Styles of Communication and Interacting Chart on Page 125 to answer the following questions:

RESPONSIBILITY QUIZ

👑 When he is given an assignment at school, home or work, how does he go about accomplishing the assignment?
Word(s)_____ Column _____

👑 How does he react when he does something wrong or makes a mistake?
Word(s)_____ Column _____

👑 How does he react when someone else does something wrong?
Word(s)_____ Column _____

👑 How does he treat his possessions (like his room, his stereo, his car, his personal belongings)?
Word(s)_____ Column _____

👑 How does he approach his future plans?
Word(s)_____ Column _____

How many descriptive words did you indicate above from each column in the chart? Were any from the first three columns? If they were you should take a serious look at discontinuing your relationship with this guy. He is not going to be your prince and he may not be anybody's prince.

DEALING WITH FEELINGS

How he reacts and his range of emotion are important for relationships. Does he respond to feelings in ways that help the relationship function better or make it worse? Many people don't deal with their feelings very well, especially teenagers, and more especially teenage guys. Feelings are too scary, or make you seem weak (especially for guys). A mature person understands that all feelings are part of being human. That includes joy, sorrow, sadness, fear, happiness, anger, love, jealousy, hate, and any others you can think of. Having any of these feelings neither makes you weak or strong. It is how you respond to and deal with the feelings that determines how strong or weak you are. Taking responsibility for feelings and learning to respond in a mature fashion is the mark of a mature person, and some-one you should want to be with. To help assess his reaction to certain situations, use the Styles of Communication and Interacting Chart on Page 125 to answer the following questions:

FEELINGS QUIZ

👑 How does he react to negative situations?
Word(s)_____Column _____

👑 How does he defend himself, especially when he feels attacked?
Word(s)_____Column _____

👑 How does he stand up for himself?
Word(s)_____Column _____

👑 How does he treat you when he is upset or when he thinks you have offended him?
Word(s)_____Column _____

👑 How does he treat his family when he is upset?
Word(s)_____Column _____

👑 How would you describe him when he is in a good mood?
Word(s)_____Column _____

How many descriptive words did you indicate above from each column in the chart? Were any from the first three columns? We're going to say it again, if they were you should take a serious look at discontinuing your relationship with this guy. He is not going to be your prince and he may not be anybody's prince.

REMEMBERING THE LITTLE THINGS, AS WELL AS THE BIG

Another great thing to practice while dating is paying attention to the little things he does and that you can do for him. Neglecting the little things can lead to big problems. The little things set princes and princesses apart from the rest of the frogs. Remembering the little things means you are interested in the other person. It means you are willing to put in the effort to make a relationship work. It means you care. It means you pay attention and expect to be paid attention to. If the guy you are dating consistently neglects the little things, he may not be as princely as you thought. What are the little things? It's having your prince remember important dates to you, walk you to the door, put notes in your lunch box, ask you how your day went, pick a flower for you on the way in the house, wash your car without you asking, rub your feet when it's been a particularly stressful day and so on. Remember to be grateful for the little things he does and to always look for little things to do for him too.

OTHER THINGS TO CONSIDER

Use the Styles of Communication and Interacting Chart on Page 125 to answer the following questions:

OTHER THINGS TO CONSIDER QUIZ

👑 When you go out how would you describe his manners?
Word(s_____Column_____

👑 Describe his behavior when working things out with you.
Word(s_____Column_____

👑 How does he act when calling you for dates?
Word(s_____Column_____

👑 How would you describe the respect he has regarding not pushing you for more physical affection than you are comfortable with?
Word(s_____Column_____

👑 When interacting with your family, describe his behavior.
Word(s_____Column_____

👑 Does he open the door for you?
Yes _____   No _____ (a "no" answer is a bad sign)

👑 Does he come to the door to pick you up rather than honking for you out front?
Yes _____   No _____ (a "no" answer is a bad sign)

👑 When interacting with your family, describe his behavior.
Word(s_____Column_____

👑 Does he walk you to the door instead of dropping you at the curb?
Yes _____   No _____ (a "no" answer is a bad sign)

👑 Does he treat you with kindness and respect?
Yes _____   No _____ (a "no" answer is a bad sign)

👑 Does he act like he owns you?
Yes _____   No _____ (a "no" answer is a bad sign)

👑 Does he treat you like a friend and listen to and communicate with you?
Yes _____   No _____ (a "no" answer is a bad sign)

👑 Does he seem to take you for granted?
Yes _____   No _____ (a "yes" answer is a bad sign)

👑 Does he want you to see other guys?
Yes _____   No _____ (a "yes" answer is a bad sign)

👑 Does he want you to not see your friends?
Yes _____   No _____ (a "yes" answer is a bad sign)

OPPOSITES ATTRACT
BUT CAN THEY MAKE IT WORK?

ow that you really like him and think he's a prince, the issue of whether he's compatible with you presents itself. Since you continue to date him, you already think you and he are compatible. You should be asking yourself how much like you he really is. Many times girls are attracted to guys because they have certain traits that are different or opposite of theirs. Although it is true that often opposites attract, it can become a problem in long-term relationships.

Initially his opposite traits may be attractive. He is new, exciting and different from what you are used to. As the relationship progresses, however, more often than not, the traits start to irritate you. You begin to think, "Why can't he be more like this or that." Pretty soon, the very trait(s) that was so attractive to you is the cause of disagreements and arguments.

Let's take a look at an example. Hannah and Mark were very different in many ways. But they were very attracted to each other from the moment they met. Hannah had grown up in a family with many rules and expectations. They expected her to do well in school and to take care of her home responsibilities. Mark had grown up in a family where there were few rules and you could do pretty much what you wanted as long as you stayed out of trouble. Hannah found Mark's free spirit to be exciting and exhilarating. She liked Mark's carefree attitude. He was also very spontaneous and did whatever he wanted when he wanted. She liked the freedom that it gave them. Mark thought Hannah was very good looking and thought that her conservative nature was nice but somewhat old-fashioned. He relished the challenge of teaching her a "new way," even though he never told her this. She was a change of pace from the girls he had been dating.

Hannah and Mark got along very well for months. They liked being with each other and doing things together. Often Mark would call Hannah at the last minute and suggest going someplace. She found this fun, but her parents didn't like it much. This didn't slow her down, she just thought her parents were old fashioned. After a few months, Hannah's grades began to slip and she stopped going out with her female friends because she wanted to be available for Mark if he should call. It didn't take too much longer before Mark's whimsical ways started to bother Hannah. She didn't like to get bad grades. She wanted to go to college and knew how important good grades were. She also didn't like not spending time with her other friends. When she brought this up to Mark, and told him she wanted him to be more considerate by asking her out or planning their dates in advance, Mark complained that this would cramp his style. When she insisted, they had an argument. They made up, had more fights, made up, and had more arguments, almost always about the same things. Not too long after they broke up for good. Hannah and Mark both learned a lesson about opposites attracting.

Hannah and Mark's story helps illustrate a fairly common process when two people get together who have opposite character traits. There are certain traits that are more problematic than others when it comes to opposites attracting. Some of these are intelligence, education, religious beliefs, political viewpoints, income levels, views on how to handle money, cultural differences and personality differences (flamboyant and gregarious vs. shy and withdrawn).

It is true that couples have had successful relationships even though they have had one or two of these opposites or contrasting characteristics. But the odds are against you. And even with the best of relationships, if these traits are in contrast in a marriage, it takes significant work to overcome the differences. Although these issues are only a few examples of many, they are typical of the kinds of issues you will have to be aware of as you work things out in your "steady" relationship.

For example, Wendy and Josh differed in their intelligence and level of education. Wendy was quite a bit more educated and had a much more developed vocabulary than Josh. Josh found this intriguing when they were courting. It made him feel good to be with such a smart woman. However, almost every time they tried to have a discussion about something or had a disagreement Wendy would use big words and if Josh didn't understand the word, she would make remarks that made him feel like he was stupid. When Josh tried to use big words, he inevitably misused the word. Again she would correct him with a little sneer.

When they were dating Josh didn't pay too much attention to this process, thinking it was just something that he would get used to, and in the back of his mind he thought that perhaps he would learn from Wendy and be able to be equal to her intelligence. But after they married, the same pattern continued and he never seemed to be able to measure up. Eventually, Josh began to feel inferior. Feeling inferior was not something he liked so he tried all the harder to win arguments. He hated to lose. (Remember what we explained about men needing to win) What he soon resorted to was cutting Wendy down by calling her names or yelling, and eventually he even became violent on occasion. Now Josh was not a stupid man by any means, but the difference in levels of education, along with an insensitivity and insecurity on Wendy's part, ended up causing problems in the relationship. They ended up with a very conflicted relationship and neither one of them was happy with the marriage.

The thing to learn from this section is that if you find yourself attracted to someone because he is so "different" from other guys, then you should understand what you are actually attracted to. If it turns out to be an "opposite" trait realize that it could backfire on you in the long run. If you should choose to date someone with whom you differ on significant issues it may be exciting for a while, but experience shows that those differences will be problematic to the relationship. No guy will have all the same or even similar traits as you. You don't really want that. But the major areas just mentioned as well as your view on life and your expectations and goals for the future should be similar.

THINGS TO WORK ON WHEN YOU DATE FOR SERIOUS

s you get more serious with your dates you should be more and more scrutinizing. The following is a partial list of the things you should be looking at, paying attention to and asking yourself with the guys you keep accepting dates with:

- ♛ Why am I dating him?

- ♛ What are his values?

- ♛ What does he want out of life?

- ♛ He doesn't have to be everything I want, or perfect, just what I want regarding the things that are important to me.

- ♛ What is his religious and spiritual point of view? Is it similar to mine? History shows that differences in this area tend to bring disagreement and conflict later in the relationship.

- ♛ Does he want children? If so, how many? Are his desires compatible with mine?

- ♛ Does he have a child-rearing philosophy? If so what is it? If not, discuss it.

- ♛ What are his career goals? Are they acceptable or agreeable to me? (For example, you don't want to marry someone who wants to be a teacher if you expect to live a life that will require the salary of a corporate president.)

- ♛ What are his ambitions and dreams?

- ♛ Can I support him in his dreams?

- ♛ Will he support me in my ambitions and dreams?

- ♛ Is he a hard worker? It takes a lot of hard work to make a life for a family.

- ♛ How does he feel about money? Is he a free spender or is he cautious with his money? Which one am I?

- ♛ Where does he want to live? Is it compatible with where I want to live?

- ♛ What are his relationships like with his family?

- ♛ What do his relationships say about his ability to have a good healthy relationship?

- ♛ How important is it to him to maintain relationships with his friends? How much time will that take?

- ♛ What does "success" mean to him? Does it include all aspects of success such as happy home, business, professional, friends, church, civic, etc.

- ♛ What are his beliefs about what a long-term, committed relationship is? Is he willing to work to change and grow with the relationship? Remember, everyone grows and changes over time. If both of you are not willing to grow with and adjust to each other, a long-term relationship will be very difficult to uphold.

- ♛ How does he define love and how do I fit into that definition?

- ♛ Does he take care of his health, both physical and emotional?

- ♛ What are his hobbies? What does he like to do in his spare time? Does he use it in a productive way or does he tend to "chill" or vegetate in front of the TV?

♛ Is he honest, trusting of me, and trusting of others

♛ Is he caring, and kind?

♛ Does he believe in equality of the sexes, in sharing roles equally, and in treating me like an equal partner?

♛ Is he interested in self-development and improvement?

♛ Is he self-oriented, always thinking himself and what he can get from a situation? Or does he consider others and their needs as well?

If you don't know these things about him, and you haven't shared the way you feel about these issues with him, begin to have these discussions. No one should steady date someone for very long, without exchanging their views on these important issues. This process of understanding does not have to be like an investigation or interview process. These topics should come up in normal conversation and by observing how he acts and treats others.

QUESTIONS TO ASK YOURSELF BEFORE COMMITTING FURTHER

n addition to the questions above to consider while you are dating. Here are in-depth questions you should know or ask your steady dates, along with hints on why the answer is so important. They include questions about his family of origin. Few other aspects of life are more important than what we were taught by those who raised us. Our upbringing affects us in countless ways, and many of these effects remain unknown to us. Our families influence, usually unconsciously, how we think, whom we find attractive, whom we choose to be with, how we act, and how we interact with others.

Question: How does he treat people he doesn't "have" to be nice to (people who hold no power over him)? These include children, the elderly, other drivers, people who are not around (does he talk behind their backs?) and especially ex-girlfriends.

Hint: A person who only treats people well if they can "do" something for him, is displaying a very "froggy" personality trait. It shows a person who is self-interested and who looks at people as if they are objects whose purpose is to serve him. What often happens is he will come to treat you in the same way. Since all relationships lose some of the hormone-fueled thrill over time, he will tend to be reluctant to do the work necessary to keep the relationship alive after the first tingle fades (see the discussion on "Crushes in Chapter 4). All relationships need continual care if they are to survive and flourish. It makes it almost impossible to make a marriage work if he doesn't value you beyond what you can do for him.

Question: Does he tend to look for the best in people?

Hint: If he is cynical and negative, it will become very easy for him to eventually look for the negative in you. All of us have negative personality traits. It takes no special talent to find the weaknesses in others or in situations in life. The fact that he has a negative outlook toward life will not mean a relationship cannot work with this man, it just makes it harder.

Question: Is he honest? Is he honest generally?

Hint: If he's dishonest with others, chances are high he will eventually be dishonest with you. There's a pattern. He may seem like he will treat you differently than he treats all other people, but the chances of that become smaller and smaller as the relationship progresses. Does he cut corners in business? Does he cheat in school? Does he call in to work sick, then go golfing? Does he tell "minor" lies in order to cover his tracks? If he does things like this habitually, you will almost always find this behavior will be part of your relationship.

Question: How does he deal with anger?

Hint: Anger is not a forbidden emotion. We all become angry. The important thing is how appropriately we deal with anger. If the guy you are dating becomes violent or abusive verbally or physically when he is angry, you should rethink your relationship with him. If a guy is violent with you before you are married, research on family violence shows that these men tend to become even more, not less, violent after marriage. Many women believe that, "if I just show my commitment to him and love him enough after we're married, he won't have any excuse to be angry or violent." But men who are violent do not need any excuse to be violent, because the violence comes from within them—from their insecurities, their low self-esteem, their lack of skills for dealing with life events, and from lack of self-discipline to not be violent though they feel like striking out. Events in the home or family can create a situation where he becomes more violent or is violent more often. His violence is his responsibility, not yours. He needs to get help to get his violent behavior under control.

Question: How does he deal with frustration?

Hint: Life in general brings countless frustrations. Moreover, long-term relationships also require a great deal of discussion and negotiation. If a guy you are dating deals with frustration by becoming uncontrollably angry, this is a bad sign. If, on the other hand, he deals with frustration by becoming angry, then calming down, then problem-solving, he is much more likely to work together with you on the problems you will face together as a couple.

Question: Is he willing to show you his vulnerability?

Hint: Showing emotional vulnerability is hard for almost everyone, and usually harder for men. However, if he never shows emotional sensitivity at some interval throughout your relationship, we believe you will have great difficulty reaching the most important goal of all close relationships—a profound connection to another human being. If he has trouble opening up to you and showing his vulnerability even after you are in a committed, steady dating relationship, you might suggest to your guy that he work on being more open. Some times this is best accomplished with the help of a professional therapist.

Question: Does he listen to you?

Hint: Women tend to be, on average, more verbally skilled than men. This is one of the most thoroughly documented gender differences of all, and one of the most frustrating differences between men and women. But, although it may not be easy for men to communicate effectively with their female partners, they should still put in the effort necessary to learn this critical skill. They may never learn to communicate as well as a "kindred spirit" girlfriend may, but they can learn to listen and validate your feelings and concerns. It is a bad sign when your guy doesn't even try to do this much in the relationship, especially while you are steady dating.

Question: Does he promise marriage when he's "ready"?

Hint: There is a point when both of you know it is time to start talking about marriage. You can sense it. You can tell that if you don't discuss a long-term commitment, the relationship will grow stagnant. You understand that if you put off taking the next step, valuable time is being wasted—time you could spend either deepening your relationship with your partner or looking for someone else. While there is no "required" time when people who have been dating should start to plan marriage, it is counterproductive to become so comfortable in a relationship that one or both partners begin to take the relationship for granted. This happens when there is no clear sense of commitment. If you both understand that you should have this talk, and he is unwilling or he tells you he will commit "when he is ready," he may have trouble committing. This difficulty committing applies not only to a more serious relationship with you, but with emotional intimacy in general. Almost everyone who dates for very long will eventually be aware of the point in time when this discussion should take place. If you know it's time, and he is still trying to "find the right moment," bring this up with him. If you are unable to come to an understanding that is acceptable to both of you, then it may be a good idea to attend couples counseling together, especially if you think marriage is a what you want from the relationship.

Question: How does he feel about children? How many? What are his ideas regarding discipline?

Hint: This is one of the big issues. If he likes to be around children and treats them well, chances are that he will be a better sort of father to your children. If having children is important to you, you want to marry someone who has the same desire. You should also agree to the number of children you want. Couples who disagree on the number of children can have very difficult marriages.

Question: Do you tell yourself he will change if only I love him enough?

Hint: A person, male or female, rarely changes just because his or her partner keeps "giving" in the relationship. More often, that partner continues to take more and more, finally leaving his or her partner emotionally exhausted and humiliated. It is somewhat like when you have a bank account. If you make deposits, you will have money to withdraw when you need to buy or pay for something. As long as you make deposits, you have money to withdraw, and as long as you deposit more than you withdraw you will always have reserve in times of emergency. If, on the other hand, all you do is make withdrawals, you will have nothing left and you will be in debt. Relationships are like emotional bank accounts. You need to make emotional deposits such as doing love things, giving compliments, fulfilling your responsibilities in the relationship, apologizing when wrong, etc., so that when difficulties come up you are not making withdrawals on an empty account. If one or both of you do not make deposits, it will leave the other emotionally depleted and exhausted.

People change—this is inevitable. But the big question is whether this change makes them easier to live with or not. With this in mind, here's a general rule for dating and marriage: if a partner acts a certain way before the marriage, he or she will tend to act the same way after marriage, only more so. If your guy doesn't continually make emotional deposits into the relationship account before you get married, it is likely that he will make even less after getting married.

Question: Has he used drugs and, if so, is he still using?

Hint: If he has used drugs, how long has he been clean and sober? If he is currently using drugs, there will likely be many repercussions from this usage, nearly all of them bad. These problems can include mood swings, financial problems, employment problems, and the most common trait of all, telling lies. People who use drugs are forced to lie because they are doing something illegal on a consistent basis. They are living a lie, and they can't be honest about other things in their lives. There isn't anyone with existing drug and alcohol problems whose professional and emotional lives are in order. They may seem that they are functional, but sooner or later you have to pay the piper, so to speak. It will eventually catch up with them. If your boyfriend or you are using drugs, it is not a very good foundation upon which to build a relationship. Take steps to stop using and deal with the emotional issues that makes using drugs the way you cope with life. It should be pointed out that many recovering drug and alcohol abusers have turned their lives around and make marvelously reliable employees and husbands/fathers, but don't get involved thinking he will change.

Question: How was discipline handled in his family?

Hint: This question is very important because we all tend to treat our children in much the same way we were treated by our own parents. It is possible to treat our children differently than we were treated, but this usually takes a tremendous amount of effort to accomplish. What's more, many of the traits we most want to avoid as a parent will not present themselves until our children become old enough to have their own opinions (usually some time between 2 and 3 1/2 years old). Discuss the question of child-discipline with your partner and try to come to an agreement before you have children. You don't want to have to decide what to do after your toddler throws his bowl of cereal on the floor in a rage.

Question: How did his family deal with strong emotion—especially anger and feelings of hurt?

Hint: It is important that families allow a range of emotional expression in the family. As mentioned, it is natural for human beings to experience strong emotion. It is unnatural for parents to try to convince children that they should not feel these emotions. These feelings go somewhere. Where do they go? These emotions settle down deep within the psyche if they aren't expressed appropriately. They then often emerge in adolescence or adulthood in various ways. They can appear as rage, or as a defensive and blaming personality. They can also appear in more serious forms such as drug and alcohol addictions, workaholism, kleptomania (stealing uncontrollably), gambling addictions, sex or pornography addictions, eating disorders such as bulimia or anorexia, or a preoccupation with sports, video games, television, computer projects, car projects, or any other activity that interferes with relationships and normal life functioning. Some of these activities are not negative in and of themselves but, taken to an extreme, each of them can make a good relationship extremely difficult.

Question: How was sex dealt with in his family?

Hint: Was it stuffed or repressed? Was it ignored or avoided? Did they talk about it with respect, or did they just let the schools teach the kids about it? Sexuality is a normal, natural, and healthy part of being human. Parents ignore these feelings which are developing in their children at their own peril. If parents refuse to teach their children about sexuality or actively repress it and call it dirty, they will drive these enormously powerful feelings underground. The feelings will come back later disguised as a variety of problems. On the other hand, it is a very good sign if the family of the guy you are dating was open and had a healthy, though not obsessive, view of the nature of human sexuality. They should have treated it as something to be careful with and treasured, not as something to fear and ignore. Sex is beautiful and should be treated as such. When it is obsessed about or treated as just something for your pleasure and entertainment, it becomes less than it should be. If you or your boyfriend see sex as merely a good time and something that all kids do, then you are not giving it the respect it is due.

Question: Does he feel he was neglected or ignored by his parents?

Hint: If the guy you are dating felt ignored or neglected, either emotionally or physically, as he was growing up, there are several issues for him to resolve. Adults ignored as children generally struggle with fundamental doubts about their worth as people. This may lead to a variety of problems including depression, a lack of ambition or, conversely, an obsession with achievement (to prove their worth). If they are depressed, they may retreat into a variety of activities, including drug and alcohol abuse, incessant preoccupation with hobbies such as automobiles, television, sports, pornography, video-games, Internet, or computer activities. These men may also have trouble giving emotional intimacy to those in their family, including you and his children. It is very hard to give love and nurturing if a person didn't feel love and nurturing when he or she was a child.

Although the fact that your guy was not nurtured as a child brings added difficulty for making relationships work, it is an issue that can be addressed satisfactorily, especially with a good therapist. The important element of dealing with this issue is for this "adult boy" to learn to recognize the feelings he is trying to avoid when he "disappears into the shop," or spends hours on a weekend television-watching or video-game-playing binge, or gets angry at things that don't seem to really matter. These feelings often include worthlessness, powerlessness, sadness, anger and abandonment. The next step in resolving these feelings is to turn to people who care about them when they begin to feel dejected or depressed.

Question: How were women treated in the family?

Hint: Were women second-class citizens? Expected to serve men? Or, were they overindulged and treated better than the male family members? If either of these was the case, it is important to discuss and work out these issues. Both of you should agree on the roles men and women will play in your marriage. Spend some time discussing this issue with him and watch closely to see whether his behavior matches what he says. The hard part about his view of women is that it might not be obvious. Even he might not be able to tell you how he feels about women in general. But over time, his behavior is the surest sign of his inner views. How does he respond when women are powerful or have authority? What does he think of your opinions? Does he listen to them and give them respect?

Question: What does he think of his parents?

Hint: Does he hate or dislike his parents to an extreme degree? If this is so, there is a reason he dislikes them, even if the reason may be partially due to his problems. But whether the problems are due to his parents, him and his personality, or some combination of the two, counseling can help you both understand and deal with them before you make the commitment of marriage.

Question: What was his parents' relationship like?

Hint: Did he have good role models to follow? Did he have a good relationship to pattern his own relationships after? Were his parents kind to each other? Did he witness abuse? These are all questions you should explore before you commit to an ongoing relationship with him. And again, it is more important that he is willing to work on becoming different than his parents rather than expect him to not have any negative issues regarding his parents.

Question: Was there drug or alcohol abuse in the family?

Hint: If there was drug or alcohol abuse in his family, it will be very helpful to you to consult books on Adult Children of Alcoholics. Growing up in a home like this creates many problems unique to these families and these problems make creating a new family all the more difficult (although certainly not impossible). The books available on the subject are generally quite excellent. Check into your local library or bookstore for additional help.

Question: Was there abuse in his family: physical, emotional or sexual?

Hint: Physical abuse (hitting, beating, harsh discipline) creates a great variety of problems, most frequently a rage that can seem irrational but which is understandable given what happened to an abused child. This rage may be played out in a number of ways. He may rebel at "authority" or refuse to follow rules, because authority and rules never protected him, and those in authority over him caused him pain. He may also be hypersensitive to issues of justice and fairness, which is not a bad thing in and of itself, except that victims of abuse tend to obsess over everyone "getting exactly what they deserve." They often become the "guardians of justice" and refuse to leave issues alone, even small ones. They can be emotionally exhausting partners to be with because nearly every event is a major issue to them. They have a hard time letting things go, even if they can admit that the issue is really not worth all the energy put into it. This is not to say that anyone who has been abused is guaranteed to have these problems, just that it is more likely.

Of course, one of the most common and dangerous effects of those who were physically abused as kids is tendency for them to resort to abusive behavior themselves with their wives and, more commonly, their children. Abuse can be defined as any intentionally harmful physical contact. This includes hitting or punching, slapping, kicking, choking, biting, throwing objects, shoving or pushing (even if it is up against a wall). Physical abuse can also be defined as restraining, or physically preventing someone from leaving a room or a house, including standing in the way of someone who wants to leave, blocking a doorway or holding onto a wrist or another part of the body. You must take your chances of his committing abuse if he was abused and has never worked through it with a professional therapist.

If there was physical abuse in the family, there was almost certainly emotional/verbal abuse as well. Emotional/verbal abuse involves screaming, yelling, humiliating or shaming behavior, name calling, insults, ignoring, put-downs, etc. The effects of emotional/verbal abuse on the victims include fear of failure, low self-esteem, difficulty coping with strong emotion, and difficulty trusting others. You should ask the guy you are dating how his parents treated him so that you can work through these issues before you have to deal with them within a marriage.

If there was sexual abuse in his family, it is recommended that he see a professional therapist who has experience with these issues. Rather than give too little information about this issue, we would rather refer you to several books on the subject. There are numerous effects on adults who were abused sexually as children such as a reluctance to engage in sexual activity or, just the opposite, an obsession with sexual activity. Sexuality in victims of sexual abuse is almost always distorted in important ways. This does NOT mean that these survivors of sexual abuse are not worthy of your love. It only means that there are almost certainly issues regarding sexuality that should be resolved with a professional therapist. It can also mean a long-term healing and growth process that requires professional help. There is almost always an emotional distance that is difficult to understand for the partner who is not a victim. Much understanding and patience is required should your boyfriend or you be a victim of sexual abuse.

IMPERFECTION: FROG TRAITS YOU MIGHT BE ABLE TO LIVE WITH

 emember no man is perfect (or woman for that matter). Happy marriages are made up of imperfect and growing people. There are certain character traits which might not be the best to live with, but which, if he is princely in other ways, would probably be acceptable. After all, we don't want you to throw away a good guy just because he displays the traits that almost all men display.

Typical "guy" issues you can get by with:

👑 A "reasonable" amount of playing or watching sports. Men tend to be competitive and sports helps fulfill that need. If they spend the whole day in front of the TV that could be a problem, especially if he has no particular connection to the teams. It could also be a problem if he watches games to the exclusion of getting other things done around the house or other life responsibilities. But if he is a sports buff, that is not necessarily a frog sign.

♛ Being mildly distracted while you are trying to talk to him. He is probably paying attention but you may see it as not listening. Men communicate differently than women. Understanding the difference will help you feel that you are communicating, it just may not be how you would like it to be. Try to understand how he communicates so you can pick up on his style. He should be encouraged to do the same for you.

♛ Lapses in cleanliness. It may not be OK to be sloppy, it may drive you crazy. But most men are less neat than women. That does not mean they are going to be impossible to live with. You may need to make some adjustment in your expectations of cleanliness and neatness. But you don't need to lower your standards. This is something that can easily be addressed between the two of you if both of you are willing to work on making the relationship work.

♛ Forgetfulness at times. Forgetting anniversary dates and birthdays, etc., might seem totally inconsiderate to you but it may just be an oversight on his part. It doesn't necessarily mean he doesn't value the day or you or the relationship. Men, in general, place different meaning on special dates than most women. It is something that you may have to train him to pay attention to. If he values the relationship then he will make adjustments and try harder. Also something that you can do to avoid his forgetfulness is to remind him. Don't just think, "If he really cares he will remember." Take the initiative to let him know a certain important date is coming up. Which is better, to remind him and have him pay attention to you and have a good time, or see if he remembers and if he doesn't to then be mad at him and have a horrible time or worse yet, no time at all?

♛ Some laziness- what you might see as lazy may just be a difference in timing. If, on the other hand, he doesn't complete his responsibilities he truly could be lazy. But if it usually gets done it may indicate that he is operating on a different time line than you. Give him the space to be his own person, but watch out for patterns of irresponsibility.

♛ Moderate procrastination- Sometimes, these last two can be understood as reflecting a different timeline than you have. It might have something to do with who he is, but it usually indicates a difference in priorities. Let him do things on his own schedule as long as it gets done. What you might find is that if you back off he will actually do it on his own. It has something to do with the winning thing we talked about in Chapter 4.

SIGNS HE MIGHT BE RIGHT FOR YOU

 s he right for you? This is the question that everyone in a close dating relationship would like to know. While no one on earth can answer this question for you directly, hopefully, the following signs can help you:

- The relationship feels very "natural" when you are with him. Not everything is a battle when you are together. Things seem to "flow."

- You feel like your values are roughly the same. You seem to agree with the way he runs his life in general. Opposites may attract with physical traits and emotional temperament but they should NOT with goals and values.

- You feel equally mature. You aren't embarrassed by his behavior and he's not embarrassed by yours. Girls tend to see some male behavior as childish, especially in late adolescence or early adulthood. Guys seem to mature slower than girls. They, by nature, love to play, and it is a bigger part of their world than it is for girls. With that in mind, if you still feel equally mature, it is a good sign.

- You find yourself wanting to be a better person when you are with him but not because he acts like he's superior to you. It's more that you feel like he's such a good man that he inspires you to want to become better.

- He encourages you to build yourself and develop your talents and abilities.

- He encourages you to seek to fulfill your dreams.

- He treats you with respect, even if you disagree with him.

- He shows interest in your activities. He attends them and takes an active interest in your part in them.

- Most of your questions in the previous activities indicate a trait from the 4th column in the Styles of Communication Chart on Page 125.

FOR THE RELIGIOUSLY-ORIENTED READER

If the spiritual aspect of life is important to you, we recommend you do two things before you decide to forge a long-term relationship with the person you have been dating: 1) take the question to your local spiritual advisor, and 2) take the question to God in prayer.

This is an important thing to do if you are religious. Your God is the most important being in your life, especially as it pertains to your happiness and well being.

Your spiritual leaders want the best for you as well. He or she should be able to give you valuable insight and guidance. They can help you avoid a lot of hurt and trouble by giving you good advice.

SIGNS IT'S HEADED FOR DISASTER

 he following are signs that your relationship is not built upon aspects of character (yours or his) that are important enough to help you in your relationship:

- You spend most of your time talking to him about his problems.

- He claims that you are the only one who has ever truly understood him.

- You find that no matter how much you try, he is never quite satisfied with you. It never seems like it is good enough. He always wants something "more" or "different" from you.

- Your greatest attraction to each other is physical or sexual.

- Your greatest attraction to each other is financial.

- After a few weeks or months he doesn't seem to pay as much attention to you.

- He says that you are the one for him and/or you have both committed to be exclusive yet he still messes around with other girls. When you confront him about this behavior he says that you are just being jealous and that they don't mean a thing to him.

- You feel so jealous of any other girl that he even notices, or that you think he notices.

♛ You try to talk to him about subjects important to you but he won't talk about them except on a superficial level

THE DARK RED FLAGS

You should consider the following to be warning signals that the guy you once thought highly of or maybe even considered a prince will not enable you to live happily ever after. If he has shown any of the following traits, please rethink your plans for a long-term relationship with him. In fact, if he has shown violence or more than even one of the following traits (even if they are non-violent), we suggest you reconsider any kind of involvement with him. Remember, that even though you are dating this guy steady, you have made no long term, engagement type commitment to him. You have no reason to stay and many to leave if some of the following are present in your relationship. This may be the most important thing in this book.

Does the guy you are dating...

♛ Use violence (hitting, pushing, restraining, blocking your path, threatening, destruction of property)?

♛ Abuse drugs or alcohol?

♛ Forbid, or attempt to restrict, you from having friends or spending time alone without him?

♛ Restrict your use of the phone?

♛ Insult you?

♛ Flirt with other girls while in your presence?

♛ Flirt with other girls when not with you?

♛ Change jobs often or fail to hold a job?

♛ Complain constantly that bosses/women/other drivers/parents, etc. "have it in" for him?

♛ Never seem satisfied no matter how much you give him?

♛ Make insulting "jokes" (use sarcasm) at your expense, or his jokes are about you and even though you laugh, it hurts?

♛ Ask you to participate in degrading sexual practices?

- Restrict you from seeing your friends, parents or siblings?

- Tell you one thing, then you find out another. In other words, does he lie to you?

- Make you feel you can never do enough or are good enough for him?

SEXUAL CONTACT WHILE STEADY DATING

f you are dating steadily, it is a pretty good bet that you are both physically attracted to each other. You will probably be tempted to engage in some physical intimacy. There are a number of reasons why you should refrain from becoming sexual with each other. We have discussed many of them in other areas in the book. Ideally you will wait to become sexually intimate until you are married. If you choose not to wait to have sex until you are married, you should understand and accept the implications and consequences on your relationship and your life.

While sexual intimacy is important to a healthy long term committed relationship, it is not a vital component of a steady dating relationship. Many steady dating relationships are built around sexual attraction rather than on the solid foundations of relationships discussed in this book. A healthy relationship cannot be built on sexual "chemistry" alone. Sexual attraction and compatibility will never be enough to get you past the hard times in a truly intimate and lasting relationship. You and your partner need much more for a relationship to last. We talk about this more in Chapter 7. Many couples with one or both partner who had physical abnormalities or injuries have built successful relationships entirely without traditional sexuality. But no successful long-term relationship has been built entirely on sexual attraction. Sex, no matter how spectacular, is simply not enough to keep a relationship together if that relationship lacks closeness and attraction on other levels.

BREAKING UP

I f you choose to go steady, if you choose to fall in love, if you choose to give yourself to another person, you are also going to have to face the inevitable: breaking up. It's been said that everyone should go through a break-up once, but you only need to do it once to learn about breaking up. The reality is that most people will go through more than one break-up, especially if you start going steady when you are a teenager.

Breaking up is part of the dating process. You should plan on it. You might even prepare yourself for it, but no matter how much you prepare you will not be prepared for how it feels. And it doesn't matter whether it is the first break-up or twenty-first, it still hurts. If you loved the guy you are breaking up with, you will experience life from a whole new perspective. It may leave you confused, wondering what went wrong, what you could have done better, what if you would have done more? You may wonder how you are ever going to make it through the next minute of life without him in it. Life may not seem worth living without him in it. Your mother may tell you that there are lots of frogs in the swamp (or fish in the sea, as it were), but that won't make you feel better. You don't want another frog, you want your frog, even it he wasn't that good for you, even if the relationship was rough, even if you know on some level that you will be better off without him. YOU STILL WANT HIM AND IT STILL HURTS!

Believe it or not, breaking up is good for you. Think back on Princess Kate. When she broke up with Jonathon, the guy with the drop-dead eyes, she was crushed. She couldn't believe that she had actually broken up with him. She had had enough of his flirting with other girls and his lame explanations like, "We're just friends", or "I was helping her with her homework." Kate was so distraught that she became depressed. She didn't feel much like a princess. She didn't feel like going out. She didn't even feel like eating. The only thing that helped was spending time with her best friend Mary. But after a while, she began to go out with friends and found that there was life after Jonathon. She would have never believed it before, but he was not the only game in town after all. She made it through the break-up and she was stronger and better for it.

Like Kate, it may not seem like breaking up can be good for you when you are in the middle of it. But look what you get out of it. You get to grow. You learn how to handle the pain of breaking up so you get stronger. You learn how to pull through the depths of depression. You get a chance to step back from the intensity of the relationship so that you can look more objectively at it and see it for what it was, not what you imagined it to be. You get to move onto other guys that will be even better.

The reason you are breaking up is because one, or both, of you do not want to be in the relationship anymore. Things change, people grow, situations develop, others get in the way, you grow tired or bored, you meet someone else who seems to have more of what you are looking for. Especially if you are young, in your teens, breaking up can be a process of learning that you are still whole even after losing a "part of you." That part of you was only a temporary attachment that was meant to be detachable. It was a part of you that you liked having there, it was comfortable and available when you wanted it and it meant you weren't alone. When detached, you felt suddenly naked, alone, vulnerable, used and let down. You will miss having the comfort of your companionship and the love you shared. But it is a replaceable part.

You will survive. Everybody goes through it. You are not alone in your experience, nor in the depth of the pain and feelings you are having. Your parents have gone through it. Your brothers and sisters, aunts and uncles have gone through it. Your girlfriends have gone through it, or will shortly. You will go on. Take it for what it is, two people going separate ways, going on with life. It didn't work out and it will be all right.

HE MAY BE FEELING THE SAME

Sometimes part of the pain you are feeling comes because you don't think he is hurting as badly as you are. You may think that he didn't feel as strongly about you as you did about him. That hurts because you feel that you gave all you had and it wasn't enough.

However, he may be going through the same thing, and maybe even deeper feelings than you are. He may not show it. He may not want you to know about it. He may jump right into a relationship with someone else. But that does not mean he isn't hurting. Guys in general, have different ways of handling their grief. Don't be fooled by his seemingly lack of pain or caring. It may be deep. You don't have to do things to make him feel any worse. You should just go through the grieving process yourself and let him handle it the way he chooses.

There will be times that he doesn't feel as badly about it as you do. He may in fact have used you. He may not have cared that much the whole time. If this is the case, then he was a frog or predator, and you are better off without him. Move on. Check out how you got involved with him, what was it that attracted you to him, why did you let yourself be fooled into thinking that he loved you like you loved him. Be honest with yourself. That is the only way to grow and learn from the experience. Try to adjust your thinking so that this doesn't happen again.

Most of all, don't be too hard on yourself. Many women (and many men for that matter) have been fooled into thinking they had a better relationship than they really had. If you learn from this experience, you will be more selective in future relationships. That's what the dating process should be about - learning to tell the frogs from the princes so that you can have good, healthy relationships in the future.

HELP FOR PARENTS

Your daughter's boyfriend will be much more likely to treat her with respect if he knows that she has parents who are watching out for her. In fact, we recommend a practice considered "quaint and outdated" by recent generations. If your daughter is under age eighteen (and maybe even older if she consents to it), we recommend that you make a special effort to get to know the guys she dates. Have them come into the house and meet you. You don't have to show him your shotgun or otherwise try to intimidate him, you only have to be pleasant and interested in his life. By doing this, you will let him know that your daughter is precious to you, that you care about her and who she dates, and that there are other people he will have to answer to if he mistreats her.

If your daughter is dating steadily, try to maintain a good relationship with her, even if you disagree with her choice in partner. If she senses you dislike her boyfriend, she will almost always choose him over you—if she is forced to choose. Remember Romeo and Juliet? If your daughter feels like you are on her side, she will listen to you more often when you tell her of your concern for the way that he is treating her. If your fears come true and he mistreats her, your daughter will be more likely to trust your wisdom. And the next time she dates, she will be much more likely to ask you for your opinion about the guy she is dating.

Some other points to consider:

♛ Be understanding. Realize that your experience is not that of your daughter. She lives in a different world than you did when you grew up. Her challenges will be different and she needs your understanding not your lecturing. Be flexible yet consistent. Let her make her own decisions, but let her know where you stand and what your feelings and values are. Flexibility does not mean changing your mind anytime it seems convenient. It means not being so rigid that you impose your life on her to the exclusion of her making her own choices in life.

- ♛ Be supportive. There will be times when you don't agree with her choices or when she rebels against you. Let her know that you don't agree, but that you love and support her and will be there for her if she needs you. Knowing this will give her a level of security that will help her make the good choices in life, even if they are difficult.

- ♛ Love her. Above all else, love her and let her know it. You don't have to like the things she does, but you should always love her. The most important thing you can do as a parent for your children is let them know that you love them, in words and in actions.

- ♛ If she is going through a break-up, be there for her. Support her in her pain. She probably feels that no one else in the whole world can understand what she is going through. Don't try to convince her that you understand. It can be helpful to tell her the story of your first break-up or of a subsequent break-up that left you hurting. She may begin to believe that you have been through something similar. But don't force it on her. Let her go through the grief process on her own terms and in her own time. With you there to support her, she will eventually come through it. Have faith in her. She is a strong girl and will come out even stronger.

- ♛ Encourage her to date many guys, even if she dates one guy more steadily than others. There is safety in this approach to dating, as we have discussed.

CHAPTER 6

OUT OF THE SWAMP, ONTO DRY GROUND: ENGAGEMENT

oo Rah! You've found him. He is your Prince Charming. You've done all you could to prepare yourself and to learn what to look for and what to avoid in a guy. You've probably made a few mistakes along the way as well. You've even gone through a couple break-ups with all the accompanying pain and grief. But now you have planted that Miracle Kiss on the one you love and Shazam!, he turned into your prince. You know it, he knows it and you both want to make it permanent. You decide that you are ready for the big step: you're going to get married so you promise yourselves to each other. You get engaged.

Getting engaged is a big step. It means a lot of changes are going to take place in your life. One of those changes is the idea that all other people in the world are no longer options for dating and mating. But before you jump headlong into the engagement, the one thing to understand about engagement is that it is exactly that, an "engagement." It means that you have promised each other to marry. It is a promise. It is betrothal. It is nothing more.

You are not yet married. You do not have the legally binding contract that accompanies marriage. As such, it is a very important time to make sure that your fiancé is not just a frog in prince's clothing, but truly is your prince. Engagement is really the ultimate time to make sure you have found your prince. It is the first time that you have officially committed to each other. You are not just dating anymore. You are checking out the possibility of making a successful, happy and fulfilling life with this guy. So engagement is just one more step, although a big one, in the process of finding your Prince Charming.

SUCCESSFUL ENGAGEMENTS

 successful engagement is one that results in a successful, long term, happy marriage, OR a break-up prior to marriage. An engagement that results in a terrible marriage is not successful at all. A broken engagement is not a failure!! It is a success. It may hurt a lot more than other break-ups because you are even more committed to each other and you have a lot invested emotionally. But it is so much better to break off an engagement than to marry and then divorce later because you didn't want to face the embarrassment or pain of breaking off the engagement. This is especially true if you saw frog signs but decided to ignore them or convinced yourself that it would all change after you married.

Willow's engagement with Jared was an example of a successful engagement that ended in calling off the marriage. When she got engaged, she just knew Jared was her Prince Charming. They had been steady dating for about a year. Everything seemed about perfect. They were totally in love and they decided that they would express that love to the world by getting married. They planned the marriage for six months in the future. Before they got engaged, they spent most of their time together. After they got engaged, they spent almost every minute together.

During their steady dating stage, there were occasional disagreements, but sometimes making up after the arguments was so sweet it almost made the arguments worth it. The fights were usually about what Jared thought they ought to do or who they should hang out with. Even though it caused disagreements, Willow didn't think it was any big deal so she just let it go. After about two months of engagement, though, Willow began to notice that she was feeling a little crowded. Jared was making demands on her that he never had before. He began telling her how she should spend her money. He explained that now it was their money and he should have a say in how she spent it. He began to be less interested in going out to do fun things. He wanted to stay at home at his or her apartment and watch TV or videos.

She noticed that she became less patient with Jared. She didn't like many of the things he did. She had noticed them before, but now they began to be irritating to her. For instance, she didn't like the way he always "dressed down" and wore sweat pants when he was with her. She tried to get him to wear nicer clothes, but he would say that it was how he liked to dress. At first she would just let it go but she grew more and more bothered by that as well as other things.

As she grew impatient she began to make her own demands on Jared. He didn't take these demands very well and would get upset with her. Jared started acting jealous. He didn't want her to see old friends. He said that he should be enough for her and that they needed to spend their engagement with each other. At first Willow accepted his explanation and agreed to not see her friends. After a while, however, she realized just how much she missed them.

Pretty soon she began to recognize some of the signs of a frog emerging in Jared. She was very surprised, because she had been so sure that he was her prince before they got engaged. It seemed the more she tried to stay the same as she was (see her friends, do the activities that she had enjoyed, spend time with her family) the more irritated Jared became. They fought more often.

Finally, after about four months of engagement, she was talking to her mother one night about her relationship and impending marriage. She explained how she felt and that she was having second thoughts about getting married. Her mother told her that she might just be getting cold feet and that was normal.

When Willow continued telling about her feelings, her mother, who to this point had been trying to stay out of the way, finally told Willow that she had noticed that Willow didn't seem the same since the engagement. Instead of being excited and energetic, she was distant, aloof, and even seemed depressed. When Willow heard this from her mother, a light went off in her head and she too realized that she wasn't very happy, and she had a very good idea why.

She decided to talk to Jared about how she was feeling. When she explained her feelings to him he went ballistic, throwing a huge fit. He started yelling at her and told her that she was a selfish witch, and claimed that her mother and friends had made her think this way. He demanded that she not see any of them again and swore that if she did they were done.

This tirade scared her. She was also worried about losing Jared, because she loved him so much. But it also opened her eyes to a side of Jared that she really hadn't wanted to admit he had. She thought it through, took courage, and told him that if that is what she had to look forward to for the rest of her life, then she didn't want to have anything to do with him. At that, she got up and left. He was so shocked that for a moment he just stood there. Then he ran after her. He said he was sorry, but she held strong and went home.

Their relationship went back and forth for another couple weeks but Willow could see that Jared had some serious flaws that were red flags for marriage. They were not the kind of things that get better after marriage, only worse. She was wise enough to see it, admit it to herself, and finally she told Jared that the engagement was off. She returned the ring and told him good-bye. She spent a lot of time crying and feeling bad about losing Jared. It was confusing to her because she knew that she was making the right decision, but it still hurt so much. She felt like a failure. At times she even thought about giving Jared another try, but she had given him many chances and it always turned out the same.

Eventually, with the help of some very good friends and some very loving parents, she got over the pain of breaking up with Jared. She had moments of doubt about whether she had made the right decision. Eventually, she was able to start dating again and slowly worked her way out of the gloom that enveloped her following the breakup. She began to feel like her old self again, and many friends mentioned that they were glad to have her back.

Willow eventually felt relieved because she knew in her heart that she had a successful engagement, even though it didn't feel like it. She could only imagine the hell she would have gone through if she would have married Jared.

She had learned some valuable lessons. She thought she knew Jared so well. When they first got engaged, he wanted to get married right away, but she wanted to wait for six months to get to know him on a different level and also so she could make adequate plans for the wedding she had always wanted. She also learned to listen to others who had noticed some of Jared's bad traits. She was so oblivious to the warning signs because she was so much in love. Now she wished she would have paid more attention to her friends and family.

Unfortunately Willow's experience is rare because she actually broke it off. Many, too many, girls, for whatever reasons, don't break off an engagement in spite of seeing frog signs. Don't fool yourself by thinking that you already know your guy. Each step along the dating path brings new perspectives, new opportunities to know each other differently. Engagement is the final big step along the dating path.

You think you know each other, but the engagement period is a chance to get to know each other even better. It is a discovery period to see if a long-term commitment makes sense. The increased commitment that comes with engagement, with promising yourselves to each other, brings added security and should bring an additional willingness to be more open and emotionally intimate with each other. The opposite also might happen. In other words, the added commitment might make you or your fiancé be even less open. If you feel the tendency to close down, it should be a sign to you that there is something troubling going on in your relationship. The typical process is that both of you will share more about yourselves, who you are, and what you want from life.

Engagement is a time that you will work out many things that perhaps weren't addressed in your relationship before. You should plan on investigating and exploring many things. After all, this is the man with whom you are going to spend the rest of your life, have children, build a future, create your own family and legacy. You want to make sure that you really know him. There will still be surprises, some good and some bad, after you get married. But the fewer surprises the better. Many newly married wives have made the statement, "He changed completely as soon as we were married." This happens sometimes due to the guy's thinking or beliefs about what marriage is. But mostly it happens because the girl did not spend enough time getting to know the real man, or didn't ask the right questions to get to know him.

To be sure that your Prince Charming doesn't turn out to be a wolf in sheep's clothing, during your engagement you should explore the issues on the next page.

- ♛ Fundamental life arrangements, such as where you will live?

- ♛ Who will work to support the marriage (You, him or both of you?)

- ♛ What religion will dominate your home and children?

- ♛ Examine long-term goals (Are your goals the same?)

- ♛ How do you plan to include family and friends in your relationship?

- ♛ How will you manage family finances?

- ♛ Do your likes and dislikes work together, or do they conflict?

- ♛ If you want children, how many children do you want?

- ♛ Who will stay at home when you have children?

- ♛ How will you discipline your children?

- ♛ Who will be responsible for the majority of the discipline? (Can you imagine yourself saying to your children after a particularly difficult day, "You just wait 'till your father gets home.") If this isn't your idea of how things are going to go in your family, then you should plan during your engagement how you want to address discipline.

- ♛ Emotional stability of your fiancé and yourself. Is he depressed a lot? Anxious? Easily stressed? Low or high self-esteem? Forgiving? Rigid in his thinking? Even-tempered? Easily Angered?

- ♛ Pay attention to your beliefs about marriage, roles and family. Are they similar or dissimilar?

- ♛ Whose family will you spend time with at holidays? If both families live close, how will you split your time between your and his family for visits?

- ♛ Is he willing to communicate openly about what he wants from the marriage, especially when you two are not getting along so well or when there is stress in either of your lives?

- ♛ Do both of your families approve of the marriage? If not, why not? Can steps be taken to minimize the issues?

- ♛ Does he continually ask you such questions as, "Do you really love me?", or "Do you really care about me?" These are problematic questions because they indicate that he has a high need for approval, which can cause problems after marriage.

♛ Does he treat you as an equal? Is his opinion more important than your opinion?

♛ Does he make excuses about why he does things or where he spends his time?

♛ Does it seem that you are the one making all the changes so you'll get along?

♛ Now that you are engaged, does he still behave in ways that help you feel better about yourself?

♛ Now that you are engaged, does he act like he owns you? If so, it is not a good sign and you should seriously examine your reasons for wanting to marry this guy.

The answers to the questions are crucial. If you haven't addressed these issues in your relationship, you definitely need to while you are engaged. You should also refer back to the list you developed in Chapter 3 to see if your partner helps or hinders your realistic dreams.

If you have addressed these points and the answers don't paint a very pretty picture, you should do some serious thinking and soul searching. If you still want to get married, you should definitely seek out some pre-marital counseling with a qualified marriage therapist who specializes in pre-marital therapy. Keep in mind that it is better not to marry than to marry out of desperation, fear of being alone, or because you will be embarrassed if you call it off.

DIFFERENT TYPES OF ENGAGEMENTS

very couple has a different type of engagement. Your engagement will be unique because you are unique. However, there are several general types of engagements, each with its own advantages and disadvantages.

SHORT, ROMANTIC ENGAGEMENT

This type of engagement lasts about 2-6 months. The couple usually spends most of their time making marriage plans, finding a place to live, attending wedding parties and in intense physical contact. Preparation consumes so much time, that this type of engagement leaves little time for exploration of many of the points discussed above.

Short, romantic type engagements can be problematic. You are caught up in the preparations for life together, for the wedding, the honeymoon and so forth. You are also so caught up in each other, in the ideal of the relationship, being totally "gah-gah" in love, that you don't see any flaws in each other. You think your love can conquer anything. You don't typically have the chance to get to see each other in different situations that might give you different perspectives of each other.

A shorter engagement may be more desirable for couples who have decided to wait until after they are married to have sexual relations. Couples tend to be much more intimate in the engagement period and sexual tensions usually increase. However, a short engagement does not give you enough time to truly get to know each other. Be wise in striking a balance between too short of an engagement and too long of an engagement. A short engagement may not give you opportunities to really get to know your partner. Too long of an engagement may make your goal of waiting for sexual relations until after marriage difficult.

Some changes that occur after engagement include:

- ♛ You have publicly promised yourselves to each other. That sets up a boundary and clarifies your relationship as being completely exclusive, both to you and to the world.

- ♛ The exclusivity is much more intense and stronger than when you were just going steady.

- ♛ The commitment to each other should bring additional security regarding how you feel about each other. It can allow you to share more of yourself, your dreams, your goals, as well as your quirks.

- ♛ You begin to see each other as belonging to each other. You are his and he is yours. That does not mean you are a possession to be owned and used in whatever way he wants to. What it means is that you each give yourselves to each other to share your life together and to help each other bring out the best in each other.

- ♛ Other suitors are no longer an option. You have made your decision to marry your man. This is going to be the case unless you break off the engagement.

You may experience other changes as well. These changes make huge differences to your life, the way you interact, the way you feel, the way you see your world. It's a big step and demands these kinds of changes.

Many marriages have been successful after a short engagement, but the odds are against you. If you choose to have a short engagement make sure you get to know your man by exploring the points raised throughout this book

LONG, SEPARATED ENGAGEMENT

This can occur when the couple lives apart for some reason. Maybe one is off to college, or works in another state. This type of engagement presents problems because it defeats the purpose of engagement and raises the questions of exclusivity in the relationship. If you are in this type of engagement, it is wise to make it long because it will allow you more opportunities to get to know each other. You would never want to have a short, separated engagement. You could be asking for some serious trouble. Even if you got married and the marriage lasted, the possibility for difficulties in the marriage increases dramatically.

Let's say for instance, that at some point in the marriage you two have a conflict where mean things are said and feelings get hurt. This is not uncommon. In fact, unfortunately, you might say it is to be expected. If you had a separated engagement, the first thing you may find yourself thinking in the moment of conflict is, "I should have gotten to know him better before I married him," or "How could he have changed so much after we got married?"

Those kinds of thoughts are the seeds of discontent. They make you doubt your decision to get married rather than deciding that you need to work on the marriage because you made the right choice. They open you up to a loss of belief that you can get what you expect from your marriage. They give you reasons to not work as hard at making the marriage work. All this would be based on the idea that you didn't spend enough time together during your engagement. Don't let this happen to you. There are enough difficulties and doubts you will experience in marriage without compounding and confusing them by not having an adequate engagement.

EXTENDED ENGAGEMENTS

For some people, this is the preferred approach to engagement and marriage preparation. In fact, some marriage therapy professionals believe you should be engaged for at least a year so that you can get to know each other in all the seasons, events, and holidays of the year. A year-long engagement, where the two of you spend most of your free time together and build a plan for your future, allows you to see each other at least once in many of the life situations that you may encounter in your life together.

Extended engagements give you the opportunity to assess your and your partner's relationship assets and liabilities. You get to experience each other's behaviors and attitudes in many varied situations. You will see how you and he behave in these situations. You will get to see if you like what you see, if you think it is a part of his personality you can live with, or if some changes need to be made, or if you need to bail out.

LOOK FOR GAPS IN HIS RESUME

A smart thing to do is to treat engagement as a job application and interview process of sorts. There are many guys whose appear to be everything a woman wants but once you get beyond the pretty exterior, you find a frog underneath. If you are with a guy who seems to be what you want, do yourself a favor and consider the following question. Are there "gaps in his resume?" Employers who are interviewing an applicant for a job look for continuity in the employment history. If there is a gap of more than several months, employers tend to inquire more closely in order to see why this person may not have been employed for this period of time. Often there are good reasons for this gap, but sometimes it is due to personal problems that need to be resolved. If you both commit to each other as relationship partners, you both owe each other the truth about important aspects of your history. If there are times in his life when he was idle for long periods (not working, not in school, not engaged in any honorable activity), this is a bad sign.

CHECK HIS REFERENCES

There is another way to find out what your potential partner is really like. Ask him to give you the names of three to five ex-girlfriends and how to reach them. Watch his reaction to your request. Chances are, if he is a real prince he will be OK with the request. He may be a bit disappointed that you don't trust him. Trust is not the issue. The issue is you trying to find out everything you can about your man, including some things that others have found that you may not have. The best way to check this out is to talk to them.

If he has a strong negative reaction, such as getting mad or flat out refusing or starting an argument or saying the relationship is over because you don't trust him, then chances are he is a frog in prince clothing. Worse yet, he may be trying to not let you find out that he is even worse than a frog, he may even be a predator. If he has a strong reaction to your reference request, beware.

After he gives you his reference list, call these past girlfriends to see how he treated them while he was dating them, why the relationship broke up and how he treated them after they broke up. Was he civil? Was he calm? Did he do things to them that bothered them or that bother you? The answer to these questions might not change the way you think about him. After all, perhaps they are bitter toward him and would give him a negative reference. And that might not be fair. On the other hand, it could be that this bitterness was justified by how he treated these girls. Whatever the truth is, take what all of them say together. It is hard to disbelieve a report if three to five women are saying the same things about a person.

WHAT YOU SHOULD WORK ON WHILE ENGAGED?

 here are many things that you can work on during your engage-ment. We have talked about some of them. But you might be wondering what you can do as a couple to increase the odds of having a great marriage.

If you want to succeed at anything in life, there are certain principles that must be followed. If you want to be an expert in math, you need to work on math. If you want to succeed in sports, you must practice and practice. Likewise, in marriage, there are certain things that you can do that will help increase your chances of success. These are principles of successful marriage and are addressed in more detail in Chapter 7. The principles need to be worked on all through your life together. But, the best time to start working on them is while you are engaged.

INCREASING YOUR CHANCES OF SUCCESS

One of the most eye-opening experiences you can have is to take him to family gatherings. See how he gets along or doesn't get along with your family. If you are not currently getting along with your family, and he doesn't either, believe it or not, that is not a good sign. Chances are you are not getting along with your family because of some rebellious reason, and sooner or later you will probably grow out of that phase of your life. You will probably want to reconnect with your family. If he does not get along with them, that could eventually cause conflict in your relationship.

Also see if your family likes him. You may not always agree with your family's assessment of your men, but others who know you well, such as your parents and siblings, can be very enlightening and informative. If they don't like your fiancé, don't get too defensive. Try to understand why they don't and see if there is any truth for their reasoning.

Pay attention to what he thinks of your family gatherings and traditions. Family gatherings and traditions are a very important aspect of successful marriage and family life. If he makes fun of gatherings or doesn't like them it could be a negative sign for your future family life. Try to find out what it is that he was uncomfortable with. But don't let this slide by as something that he will get over. It may not be and it could create conflict.

Have him meet your friends and spend time with both his and your friends together. You've probably already done some of this when you were steady dating, but since getting engaged changes your relationship, it could be very revealing, not to mention healthy, to spend time with friends. It helps you stay connected with friends. It sends a message that even though this is your guy and you are going to spend your life together, you want your friends to play an important part in your life.

Friendships are healthy and fulfilling, but if too much time is spent with friends, especially after marriage, it can harm the marriage. The key is to keep a balance. Don't completely cut yourself off from your friends. Make sure your guy understands that just because you are engaged, it does not mean that you can't see friends. If your fiancé becomes jealous or has a problem with your friends, it could be a bad sign for the relationship. Try to find out what his issues are. If he just doesn't like your friends that's one thing, but if he wants to isolate you that is a sure sign of a problem.

Another good idea is to double date when you are engaged. That may sound crazy, but there are several potential benefits to doing so. This is a good way to establish a social structure for the relationship. It can help you learn how to interact with each other when you are with others. That may sound like something you should already know, but engagement does change your relationship. You need to learn how to interact with others as an engaged couple.

Likewise, if you find that you don't want him to spend time with his friends, that says a lot about you and how you are in a relationship. If you find you are doing some of the things talked about here, you should definitely go back to Chapter 2 and work on yourself before you get married.

For more information about this, check out the books listed at the end of the chapter. They are very good, and should be helpful to you when making such a big decision as getting married.

THE LAST LEAP

E ngagement can be a wonderful and exciting time of your life. Keep in mind that it is a serious time too. It is a time to get to know each other more deeply than before because you have committed to each other. It is the last chance you will have to make sure you have found a prince and not a frog. Use your time wisely. Build memories of love and joy. Get to know him in every situation that you possibly can. It will serve you well for the rest of your life

HELP FOR PARENTS

♛ Be excited with and for your daughter. This is a very important time in her life. She is preparing for the great adventure of marriage. It is a very exciting time. It is also a time that she will remember for the rest of her life. There is every reason to be excited and celebrate with her.

♛ Be patient. Your daughter is likely to be a bit spacey. There is so much to take care of at this time. It is difficult for even the best wedding planner to organize all the details let alone a marriage rookie like your daughter. That, combined with the plain old goofiness of being totally in love, can make for some incoherent moments. Understand and help her out.

♛ Be careful of hurtful or negative comments about her fiancé. If they marry, it could alienate you for years to come. You may feel some anxiety about her readiness or the choice she made, but keep them to yourself. If you don't agree with her choices you have probably voiced it before she got engaged. And if she didn't listen to you then she isn't likely to listen to you now. It will just make her mad at you.

♛ If she is being abused in some way you still have an obligation to protect her and warn her against the abuse. But it is a delicate situation because she will probably be defensive. She doesn't want to believe that the man she loves is capable of abusing her. But if there is abuse going on it is still better to have her mad at you now than to spend years with a guy that will bring her down.

- ♛ Help take off some of the wedding plan pressures, but don't take over. Remember it is her wedding, not yours. Be open to her wedding ideas. Keep your comments in check. You want to make sure she has the best wedding possible, but part of that is letting her be in charge as much as she wants. If you plan some part of the wedding and it goes wrong, then she will always remember that it was your plan that made her perfect day not so perfect.

- ♛ Refrain from getting in the middle of business that should stay between your daughter and her fiancé. If your daughter tries to draw you in, set a healthy stage for her and ask her to work it out with her fiancé directly. This is good advice for all couples, but it will be an important step in the communication process they have in their marriage.

- ♛ Don't compete against your daughter's soon to be in-laws. The soon to be married couple should have enough love to go around. Keep in mind that you are not losing a daughter but gaining a son.

- ♛ If your daughter says negative things about her fiancé to you, this is a bad sign. She should consider extending or breaking-off the engagement. This should be the most positive time in her life. She should be excited, though some hesitation is natural. If she is having negative thoughts, and especially if she expresses them to you, encourage her to visit with a professional marriage and family therapist before she says, "I do."

REFERENCE

Cox, Frank D. (1999), *Human Intimacy, Marriage, The Family, and its Meaning,* Eighth Edition. Wadsworth Publishing Company.

WHERE TO TURN FOR MORE INFORMATION

Larson, Jeffry H., (2000). *Should We Stay Together.* Jossey-Bass, San Francisco.

Gottman, John, & Silver, Nan. (1999). *Seven Principles For Making Marriage Work.* Crown Publishers, Inc., New York.

CHAPTER 7

AND THEY LIVED HAPPILY EVER AFTER

ou made it through the trauma of teenage dating, finding out who you are and what you want in a man. You made it through steady dating. And you even made it through your engagement. It's been an amazing ride with a lot of ups and downs, some good and some bad. Congratulations. You're married to the man of your dreams: to your Prince.

Whoa! Hold on just a minute there. Not so fast. This book is the FrogBuster, after all, not the Marriage Manual. You're not married yet. But, now is the perfect time to read this chapter. If you have worked on yourself and made wise decisions about the guys you dated, you should be very well-prepared for the information in this chapter. This chapter is going to discuss some things you should be aware of about marriage so that you will have the best chance of having a great marriage

Marriage is a beautiful thing. It is the goal of most of us who engage in the dating game. Finding someone who you want to spend the rest of your life with is what it is all about. It's what Princess Kate wanted from early on in her life. She had to go through the murky dating bog and withstand the frogs, and even some predators, before she figured out what it took to find her prince. She had to do a lot of soul searching, a lot of looking at herself, and some not-so-comfortable honest reflection. Hopefully, you have done the same.

Even after doing everything that this book has encouraged you to do— from discovering more about yourself, to understanding how to avoid frogs— when you get married, you may be surprised to find that marriage is not what you imagined it would be. Almost every person that gets married realizes this at some time early in the marriage.

Many people find marriage to be the most challenging and frustrating thing they ever experience. Others find it extremely fulfilling in spite of the challenges. But very few find it to be exactly what they thought it would be before they got married. This is due mainly to the expectations that you and your spouse have about marriage. Everybody has different expectations of what their marriage will be. These expectations come from the many life experiences we have discussed throughout this book.

People go into marriage with unspoken expectations and when things don't go according to their expectations, they think they have failed and the marriage is unsuccessful. More often than not, when this happens, they blame their spouse for not communicating well or for not living up to their expectations. They doubt whether they married the right person and start thinking that they would be better off being on their own or with somebody new.

Most of the problems with expectations are that they are seldom communicated before marriage. Sure, the two of you spend a lot of time talking about your dreams and plans. But most people have expectations about how their marriage is going to be, how their spouse is going to treat them, what their life is going to be like after marriage, and what marriage is going to do or bring to their life. These are the types of expectations that are seldom discussed. These are also the types of expectations that cause us to be less than satisfied because they do not get met. If you want your marriage experience to be fulfilling, make it a point to talk with your fiancé before you get married about these expectations. It may be an eye opening discussion for both of you.

THE GREAT MAGNIFYING GLASS

Getting married puts you and your spouse under a magnifying glass. You get to take a close look at each other and yourself. Marriage magnifies both your and your spouse's strengths and weaknesses. You get to see even more clearly the warts that both of you missed before you got married. Yes, they will be brought right out in the open.

At this point we are not going to talk much about strengths. We are going to discuss weaknesses, because typically, your strengths do not become a problem in the marriage. It is your weaknesses, your insecurities, and your fears that bring about the challenges. Marriage often brings out those weaknesses in each of you.

It can be a scary thing to realize your spouse has weaknesses. But if you take the perspective that everybody has weaknesses, you are willing to accept and love each other in spite of your weaknesses, then marriage becomes a great opportunity for personal growth. If you have the attitude that marriage is a great opportunity to overcome your weaknesses, then you will have a chance to become a better and stronger person. It is a chance to work on yourself with the help of someone who loves you, your spouse.

If you will allow it to be, marriage can be like a pearl. Pearls are formed inside oysters. The pearl is formed because of a troubling situation. A tiny grain of sand gets inside the oyster and is an irritation to the oyster. In order to sooth the irritation, the oyster begins coating it with the smooth substance. Layer upon layer of smooth covering is laid down over time. Eventually, the grain of sand becomes a pearl, a very valuable and highly sought after prize. The grain of sand becomes a pearl because of what the oyster does with it. Sometimes sand gets inside the oyster but the oyster does not produce a pearl. It all depends on what the oyster does with the grain of sand.

The sand is like our imperfections. We all have them. But like the oyster, the difference between making a pearl out of our imperfections and not making one is what we do with them. Its all a matter of perspective.

Marriage often helps us see our imperfections. It also helps us know what we need to work on. If we don't notice our imperfections, it is almost impossible for us to work on them and progress. We can make pearls out of ourselves because, like the oyster, each person has what it takes to make something smooth, refined and highly valued, like a pearl, out of our sandy imperfections. It all depends on how we choose to deal with our imperfections and challenges.

PRINCIPLES TO HELP YOU LIVE HAPPILY EVER AFTER

 f a person wants to be a professional skier there are certain principles of skiing that if followed, will assure success. A skier must learn the correct techniques of turning, anticipating turns, understanding snow and how different types of snow demand different styles of skiing. A skier must work out to be in top physical condition. A skier must practice everyday, not just during the winter months. A skier can't just practice any old way. If she wants to be the best, she must practice the correct techniques and methods so that when the time for racing comes, she will be fully prepared. It usually takes years of work and preparation to be ready for the day of competition. She should also expect some bumps. Nobody ever got to the top of the skiing world without some falls along the way.

If the skier ignores these basic principles of success, failure will almost certainly be the result. Likewise, in marriage, if you want to succeed, you must understand the foundational principles of marital success, and apply them daily. Otherwise, you are almost certain to fail.

Since we all have imperfections and weaknesses, and most of us want to work on ourselves to become better, it is important to know what to work on. Just like the skier who wants the successful outcome of winning, any venture in life has basic foundational principles that apply to the successful outcome. If these principles are followed, the chances of a successful outcome are greatly increased. Our research has uncovered 11 foundational principles of successful marriage. Knowing and applying these foundational principles can help you understand what you have to work on and how you can work on it to increase your chances of a successful marriage outcome.

The Marriage Success Principles include:

1. Making marriage an equal PARTNERSHIP where both feel equal to the other and neither person is dominant over the other.

2. Creating LOVE based on mutual care and respect, not just sex and fantasy. Love is about what you do for each other, not just how you feel about each other.

3. SPIRITUALITY is part of striving to continually do good for your self and your spouse. It is about overcoming the tendency to do things that hurt your partner, yourself and each other. Personal spiritual growth can be greatly accelerated in marriage if you work on doing good for each other and resist temptation to be angry, say mean things or hurt your spouse.

4. Total and long-term COMMITMENT to your spouse above all other relationships is critical for a successful marriage. When you get married, the search is over. You are now committed to each other and to making the marriage work. There cannot be any room for doubt or thinking about getting out of the marriage should things get difficult. A lack of commitment creates insecurity.

5. A willingness to SACRIFICE for something greater than yourself and your own selfish desires is what marriage should be all about. If you are both willing to sacrifice for the marriage you will be more likely to share yourselves more freely with each other and to achieve your mutual relationship goals together.

6. The setting of clear GOALS that both of you agree upon and are willing to work toward together. It takes some negotiation to agree upon your goals and the path to accomplish them. But once they are set, there comes a spirit of cooperation because you are headed in the same direction.

7. Respectful, clear and empathic COMMUNICATION is a must. Try your best to understand and listen to your spouse. Respect each other's point of view whether you agree with it or not. You will not always agree with each other. That is normal. But you should always respect what the other thinks or feels. Though his point of view may be different than yours, it is no less valid.

8. Taking care of your physical, emotional, spiritual, and intellectual HEALTH should be at the top of your marriage list. You can't contribute

much to a relationship if you are not healthy. If you are physically unhealthy you need to see a doctor. If you are emotionally unhealthy, you need to seek counseling and take care of it so that you can be emotionally available in the marriage. If you are not living according to your beliefs and values (like having an affair or being dishonest), you will suffer spiritually and lose strength and resolve as a person. If you are not intellectually growing, you will deteriorate and will not be as interesting to be with. Good all-around health is vital to a good life and marriage.

9. Taking RESPONSIBILITY for your behaviors and the impact you have on the success of the marriage is critical. If you find yourself saying things like, "You make me so mad," you are putting the responsibility for how you feel on the other person. You are essentially allowing them to control how you feel. No one "makes" you feel. You are the only one that makes you feel one way or another. One of the biggest problems in marital therapy is each spouse blaming the other for the problems in the marriage. They refuse to take responsibility for their own actions and want the other to be the one to blame. Once you can take responsibility for your thoughts, feelings, words, and behavior, the quality of your marriage will improve.

10. Healthy RECREATION and shared experiences continue the courtship into marriage. Doing fun things together builds the memories that make your life together special and creates those moments that you will look back on and say, "Remember the time we...." Doing fun things together helps make a vibrant relationship, and keeps variety and interest high.

11. Striking a BALANCE between all these principles and other life responsibilities to maintain a healthy life is very important. One of life's big challenges is to do everything that is demanded of you. We all have a million responsibilities. We need to prioritize and to accomplish the most important things in our life. Your marriage is the most important relationship you have in your life, and it should be at the top of your priority list. If your home life is good, then the other aspects of your life will seem easier to balance. Don't ignore your marriage and home life. If it is not going well, take the time to find out what is going on and make changes.

These concepts are the foundation of a healthy marriage. They are not always easy, but they give you the right things to think about and work on. You can build a strong, lasting marriage on these principles. If you work on these principles, you will have true romance. You will experience real love and you will love each other more after 50 years than you did when you first got married.

If you begin now and prepare yourself before you get married, most of these principles can become a natural part of your life. Build your own foundation first and it will be much easier to build your marital foundation when the time comes.

CREATING YOUR MARRIAGE

e have discussed how expectations, whether met or unmet, can bring fulfillment or dissatisfaction in marriage. We discussed how your perspective can make a big difference in how you make or don't make adjustments to your expectations in order to get the most out of your life and out of your marriage. We also discussed certain principles of successful marriages.

One of the keys to successful marriages is understanding the principles of successful marriage and then bringing your expectations out in the open together with your spouse so both of you have a better idea what each expects. Sometimes our expectations are unrealistic. Sometimes, they are unconscious. The more effort you put into making all your expectations clear to yourself and your spouse, the more likely you are to have a great marriage. That is because the two of you will have a clear understanding of the kind of marriage you each want and how you might go about getting it.

WHAT YOU SEE IS WHAT YOU GET: THE MARITAL VISION

To improve her chances of having a successful business, a business person starts with an idea or vision of what she wants to do. She then creates a business plan based on that vision and upon sound business principles. This plan improves her chances of bringing about her dream and having a successful business.

By writing her vision down and how she plans to achieve it she increases her chances to be really successful. This written plan, or vision, is called a business plan. The power of a business plan is that it clarifies her thinking. It lets others involved in the business know what she has in mind, what her expectations are, and how they can contribute in order to bring that plan to reality. It also allows the owner to check up on herself to make sure she is on track.

When two people start a business together, they form a partnership. Both partners may have different ideas about what they want the business to be, or how they want to accomplish their dreams. In order to be successful, they must clearly communicate, and negotiate those dreams, and create a written business plan that both agree on, and use each other's strengths and talents to the utmost. The reality is, and almost anyone involved in the business world will tell you, if you don't write down your dreams and plan the likelihood of succeeding goes down dramatically. So it is vitally important to write it down.

Marriage is like starting a business with a partner. Each of you has your own ideas and dreams about what a marriage is going to be. This is a good thing. These dreams and ideas need to be communicated to your partner and he needs to do the same with his dreams. Then together, you and he can discuss what those dreams and ideas are, and actually create a "marriage business plan" that both agree on, and that is based on the principles of successful marriage discussed above.

Creating a marriage business plan is the first step in creating a unified vision of what you and your future spouse want your marriage to be. But instead of calling it a marriage business plan, we call it a Marital Vision statement. You have some ideas, dreams and, yes, even fantasies about what you want your marriage to be. Creating a marital vision statement is one of the most important things you can do to make your marriage fulfilling and happy. It will help you avoid the common problem of unspoken expectations not being met.

The marital vision statement is a combination of your dream marriage and the reality of making a union between two people work. It is based on your hopes, desires, wishes, dreams and beliefs. It will be adjusted based on the fundamental principles of successful marriage.

CREATING A MARITAL VISION STATEMENT

How do you begin to create a marital vision? A marital vision is a concept and picture of what you want your marriage to be like. It is not a dream or fantasy. It is a vision that you consciously develop based on the Marriage Success Principles. The marital vision is important for marriage success because by creating it, you are establishing what you want out of a marriage. You know what you are working toward. You know what expectations you have and you have clear reasons for having them.

As a single woman, you can begin to formulate your personal marital vision statement based on the Marriage Success Principles. Then, when you find your prince, you and he can work on developing a shared marital vision. By building your foundation for building a successful marriage, you will be miles ahead of other couples who get married.

To help you start thinking about what you want in your marital vision, some examples are given below:

♔ Our marriage is based on mutual respect and love. Neither partner will make fun of the other partner for their thoughts and feelings. We do all we can to build each other up and to help each other feel good about themselves and the marriage.

♔ Our marriage is a partnership where we both feel equal. We have different talents and abilities but the combination of you and me will make us better than either of us could be alone.

♔ Our marriage is one based on doing good for each other daily, communicating respectfully, and sacrificing our own individual desires so that the mutual goals we set can be achieved together. When we don't treat each other with respect, we can let each other know by lovingly saying that we feel disrespected and the other will stop.

♔ We hope to seldom get angry with each other. We know we probably will, but we will be able to keep our anger under control without threatening each other. Even when we are angry with one another, we will not resort to calling names or putting the other down. We will never resort to violence. We will always allow each other the opportunity to take a timeout. We will always come back together to work things out when emotions are less volatile.

♔ Our marriage is based on 100% commitment. We have chosen each other for better or worse, rich or poor, sickness or health. We have given up all past relationships. While we may have feelings about past relationships, we have chosen to leave those behind and concentrate all our efforts on making this marriage work.

♔ When times of trial come into our marriage, we may feel that we want to run or leave. We understand that that is a natural response and will allow each other the space needed to work through those feelings. We know that no matter what the challenges, we will always seek each other out to work it out together.

♔ Our love is eternal. We do things daily to show that love and to make it grow. We pay attention to each other's needs and wants. We respond to those needs in ways that each likes based on what has been expressed as opposed to what we suppose is the best way.

The examples above are only partial vision statements. Your marital vision statement should include aspects of all 11 of the Marriage Success Principles.

As you probably figured from the above examples, you need to write your vision together with your husband so that you both have input and feel good about it. But you don't have to wait until you are engaged or married to develop your own statement.

When you do get engaged or married you should create your shared marital vision statement. Read it often so that you both remember the statements that will guide your marriage and help you live happily ever after (with a few bumps along the way of course).

BEYOND CROAKING: COMMUNICATING WITH YOUR PARTNER

ost people would say that good communication is the most important thing in marriage. That is not necessarily the case. As you may have figured out from the Marriage Success Principles discussed earlier, there are many aspects that create a successful marriage. They are all equally important, because if you eliminate any one then the foundation is incomplete. All must be present to have a well balanced and growth oriented marriage. However, communication is the number one complaint in marriage therapy, so we're going to cover it in a little more detail.

The first thing to understand is that the foundation of good communication is that people want to be understood, respected, and validated. They want to know that the person they are talking to respects them and will treat them with empathy and care. They want to say what is on their mind without a fear of being yelled at or put down.

You need to develop communication skills that can help you weed out the frogs in your life. Communicating clearly seems easy to do when you first fall in love with someone. You want to tell them everything. You spend all day with them and then at night you still want to be with them. You feel like you could spend every moment together. You want to share your every thought and desire with them. And they seem to do the same with you. It is a marvelous feeling.

As you spend more time together, you become more familiar with each other and the newness wears off a bit. There is less news to tell each other, and the everyday things seem to take over. Challenges come up and, believe it or not, you actually have some disagreements. You get stressed and emotions come into play. Communicating becomes a challenge when emotions are running high and stress exists.

WHY CAN IT BE DIFFICULT FOR
BOYS AND GIRLS TO COMMUNICATE?

Communicating well can be a challenge even when you are getting along. Why? Because boys and girls grow up in different ways as we discussed in Chapter 4. Women and men have different agendas when communicating. These agendas and the differences in the communication process almost always takes place on an unconscious level, so neither the man or the woman is aware of what they are doing that gets in the way of good communication.

Boys, by nature, tend to be competitive and may have a general preoccupation with winning, saving face and feeling strong. Men are more focused on independence, and being "one-up." Women, on the other hand, tend to be more focused on intimacy (connection), maintaining equality in relationships, and interdependence.[1]

When a conflict arises between a man and a woman, the woman tends to be more worried about the relationship ending or being damaged. She may try to reconcile and make all things better. A man tends to be more concerned with maintaining his status in the relationship. If the relationship goes bad it means he has failed and that makes him look weak. He will either fight for the relationship so he isn't seen as a loser, or he may withdraw so that he is less vulnerable to further attack or loss of status and loss of independence.[1]

Meanwhile, the woman sees the man's attempts to maintain his status and independence as being dominant or trying to create distance and weaken the relationship. This scares her, so she makes more attempts at making up. He sees this as a chasing him and if he gives in he may be the seen as the weak one in the relationship, so he tries harder to establish his independent status by keeping distant.[1]

Women often want to talk out a situation, and the man wants to be left alone. If things heat-up, he may even walk out of the room in mid-sentence, get mad or yell. Because he interrupts her, she feels that she must re-engage him or else she will lose the relationship. She tries harder. He distances further. She gets angry. He gets angry. She gets scared and angrier. He gets threatened and angrier still.

It can turn into a great big vicious cycle. If you understand what is going on, you can interrupt the cycle and put a stop to it before it gets out of hand. Both of you want to be understood. And both of you deserve respect and consideration. You are coming at a problem from two different perspectives, and may have two different interpretations of what the problem and the solution is.

When faced with a conflict, if you understand that he needs to have a sense of maintaining his status, it will serve you well. Some people call this letting him keep his pride, or save face. This doesn't mean that you have to give in to him and he has to win. It simply means that if you have a disagreement, a great way to show respect is to not challenge his manhood. If you make a point that seems to "win" the argument you don't need to rub it in his face or make it seem that he has lost the argument. Winning may make you feel good, but you must keep in mind that you are not in the relationship to win, you are in it to be together and to create a better life for both of you. This is where most couples fall short in their communications. They forget, or never realize, that marriage is not a competition. It is a partnership where the two of you should be working together for common objectives. In fact, if you find yourself competing in marriage, you are playing the wrong game.

Don't expect your partner to convert to your way of thinking every time. Remember that you both have a valid point of view. Solve disagreements in a way that lets each of you save face. Disagreements can actually be good. They can allow you to get closer by defining and working toward mutual goals.

SOME IDEAS TO IMPROVE YOUR INTERPERSONAL COMMUNICATION

If you are wondering how you can improve your communication both with your spouse and as well as with anyone, the following should give you some ideas for more meaningful conversations:

- ♛ Take responsibility for your actions and behaviors. The most important thing in good communication is a willingness to accept responsibility for what you do and say. Without accepting responsibility you cannot improve your interpersonal communication.

- ♛ Understand how your behaviors affect your relationship. Pay attention to the reactions of others when you say certain things. If the reaction of others is different than you were hoping for then you should consider changing how you say those things or not saying them at all.

- ♛ Change your behavior when it is detrimental to you or to your relationship.

♔ Acknowledge when you are wrong. This can be one of the best ways to avoid arguments because you show maturity and responsibility. It also eliminates the need for the other person to press his point harder to get you to "see how wrong you are."

♔ Accept that others have valid points. When you acknowledge that the person may have a point, whether you agree with it or not, creates a situation where both of you are more likely to listen to each other rather than spend your time thinking of how you are going to counter what each other is saying.

♔ Take care of issues that prevent good communication (anger, selfishness and so forth). Don't hold onto anger or old issues until it blows up all at once. Let go of it. Talk to him before it gets so ugly that a fight is unavoidable.

♔ Recognize that you may not be ready to give up some behavior, even if it would be better if you did (for instance, anger, fear of vulnerability, fear of abandonment, fear of not being OK, abuse issues).

You can change the way you approach communicating with your guy (and everyone for that matter). If you will make the following exercises part of your everyday life, others will respond more positively and be more likely to treat you with respect.

COMMUNICATION ENHANCEMENT EXERCISES

There are some sayings that you can use in place of arguing or being defensive. You may feel a little weird when you first use them. They may be very different from anything you have ever said. If you will work on them and make them part of your communication, you will find that, after a while, you will wonder how anybody gets along without them. The best time to use and practice these approaches is when there isn't any stress in the relationship. Then when there is stress it will be much easier to put them to use.

♔ "Is this the way we decided we were going to talk to each other?" (This statement is based on a decision that the two of you have made to treat each other in more positive ways. It allows your partner to stop doing what he is doing without yelling at him or condemning him. It is a reminder of how you two have previously agreed to speak with each other.)

♛ "You could be right." (This is a disarming statement. It validates the other person. It can then be followed up with your own opinion or perspective on the situation.)

♛ "I might be wrong, but it seems to me that _____." (This admits that you may not have the right or only answer and it opens up the opportunity for dialogue.)

♛ "How do you see the situation?" (This offers your partner the opportunity to voice his opinion before you throw yours at him. It says to him, Your opinion matters and I want to hear it.")

♛ "I understand how you feel. I don't necessarily agree, but you have a valid point." (This acknowledges that the other person has an opinion, it is valid, but that you have a different opinion. It doesn't imply that the other person is wrong. Nobody likes to be told they are wrong. Being told that just makes them want to argue more to prove that they are right.)

♛ "Please don't talk to me that way. When you do I feel _____." (This is clear communication of what you want—not to be treated that way, and then a statement about how you feel. This allows the other person the chance to understand and make changes. If they don't change, then you should think seriously about whether it is wise to stay in the relationship.)

♛ Use statements like, "I see," or "That's an interesting way of looking at it," or "I didn't know you saw it that way." (This is exercising empathy, trying to understand where he is coming from.) ·

♛ Learn to be a good listener (Listen to the other person until you are sure you understand. Ask them if what you heard is what they meant.)

♛ State things in terms of what you want to have or change. (Your partner cannot adjust if he doesn't know what you want. Don't make him guess.)

♛ Learn from each other (Keep in mind that you don't know everything and you can always learn something new. Be open to new information.)

♛ Listen to the tone of your voice and the authority with which you speak. Pay attention and admit it to yourself and to your spouse when you hear mean or commanding language from yourself.

- ♛ Take a marital communication class or join a communication group.

- ♛ Try something different in your communication. Stick with it even if your partner is suspicious. If it is done with good intentions meant to improve your communication process, your partner will eventually accept it.

- ♛ Emphasize what is good about you, your relationship and your communication.

- ♛ Think and talk about what you like, not what you dislike.

- ♛ Work on aspects of yourself and your relationship that you want to better.

WHEN YOU START CROAKING AT EACH OTHER: RESOLVING CONFLICT

Believe it or not, girls can croak as well as boys. Croaking at each other creates conflict. Conflict in turn creates bad feelings. Bad feelings bring resentment. Resentment brings dissatisfaction. Nobody likes any of this.

Resolving conflict is one of the biggest challenges you will face being married. If you practice the communication exercises listed above, you can resolve most, if not all, conflicts. It is good to put these in to practice prior to marriage. The following are additional things you can do to help resolve conflicts when they come up

1. Soften the start up[2] - Don't jump down his throat. If you are going to argue or disagree, try starting out with a less emotionally charged statement. Some of the statements listed above are very good for this.

2. Learn to make and receive repair attempts[2] - A repair attempt is something that a person does that tries to restore the relationship or situation to a less volatile state, to repair any damage done by the argument. Saying, "I'm sorry," is a repair attempt. Making a joke, touching gently, helping your partner, etc. are all repair attempts. Sometimes they are difficult to accept in the heat of the moment, but you should work on recognizing and accepting repair attempts by each other.

3. Soothe yourself and each other[2] - Allow yourself to relax. Step away from the conflict and do some slow breathing, take a bath, read a book or whatever helps you relax. Soothe your spouse and help him relax. Give him a massage or play relaxing music that he likes.

4. Sacrifice for the greater good of the relationship. Be willing to give up some selfish desires so that the relationship has a chance to thrive. If both you and your spouse are willing to do this, you will get more out of the relationship and life than you would had you not been willing to compromise (sacrifice) some things.

5. Be tolerant of each other's faults- Everybody has shortcomings. Nobody is perfect. Allow one another to make mistakes without assuming that it was done on purpose to hurt you.

6. Let your spouse have his dignity. (We called this "saving face" earlier.) It is always easier to resolve conflict when you feel that you are worth something and your partner feels that way too. Too often we make statements that hurt or put each other on the defensive. The statements listed above are designed to allow your spouse to have his dignity and save face in an emotionally charged situation. If you use those statements or something similar that works for you, you will find it easier to keep your own dignity and allow him to keep his as well.

All of the above approaches can be practiced prior to marriage in almost all of your close relationships, e.g., dating, family, friends, etc.

SEX, INTIMACY AND MARRIAGE

here is an old adage about sex in marriage. It goes: At first it is tri-weekly, soon it becomes try weekly and not long after that it becomes try weakly.

Most people go into marriage thinking that sex will always be great and frequent. They think it will be just like on the honeymoon. They also believe the honeymoon will last and last. Sorry to break the news. That is not usually the case.

What happens is that life gets in the way, stressors come up, kids come along, sex drives may diminish, and sex becomes less important. The challenge is to keep sex as important as both of you would like it to be.

Something to consider is that many people equate sex and intimacy. This is partly because the popular press has replaced the word "sex" with the word "intimacy." So we say, "They were intimate last night," meaning, they had sex. Real intimacy has less to do with having sex and more to do with the love that sex between loving married partners communicates to each other. Sex is a very intimate act. It is sacred and shouldn't be taken lightly. It is special and can bring you very close to your spouse. It can also tear you apart if it is abused or used to manipulate each other. It has that power. Sex opens you up to the vulnerability that we discussed earlier. It is two people sharing themselves in a very special way. This special sharing is most completely realized between two committed adults who have sworn their commitment to each other in marriage. Sex outside of marriage is less intimate. Outside of a committed marriage context, there doesn't exist the security, the level of love, the responsibility of the consequences of sex, or the spirituality. The risk of being hurt is even greater outside of the committed marriage relationship. Often, sex outside of marriage is a selfish pursuit of fulfilling one's own desires. It is not about creating a life long, loving relationship. That is why you should wait until you get married to have sex. It will help make your marriage and sexual intimacy all the more fulfilling.

Of course, you can have sex without intimacy. You can also have intimacy without sex. There have been marriages where one or both of the partners is paralyzed and has no feeling or movement below the waist. They aren't able to have sex, yet they still have a very good, fulfilling and intimate (which we define as secure emotional availability combined with mutual love and care), marriage. You can have a fulfilling marriage without sex. But you can't have a successful, fulfilling marriage without intimacy. When you combine sex and intimacy you can have a great physical and emotional relationship. Keep this in mind and you will be well on your way to having a fulfilling relationship.

HELP FOR PARENTS

- Encourage your daughter to work her problems out with her spouse. Avoid the mistake of getting involved in their relationship mishaps and struggles, especially taking sides.

- If your daughter comes to you with problems, be supportive but encourage her to work them out with her spouse

- Moving in with parents is not the greatest idea. It's hard on both couples. While it may be a great interim solution, make sure that there is a plan to move out

- Despite what we said above about getting too involved in their struggles. If you see abuse in your daughter's relationship, get involved. Help your daughter find the help she needs to resolve the conflict or get out of the relationship.

- If you don't like your daughter's spouse, keep it to yourself. She made the choice and is trying now to build a fulfilling relationship.

REFERENCES

1. Deborah Tannen, Ph.D. (1990). *You Just Don't Understand: Women and Men in Conversation.* Ballantine Books, New York.

2. Gottman, John, & Silver, Nan (1999). *The Seven Principles for Making Marriage Work.* Crown Publishers, Inc. New York.

WHERE TO TURN FOR MORE INFORMATION

Klayne Rasmussen, Ph.D. (2002). *The Common Sense Marriage.* IntraLife Systems Publishing, Utah.

CHAPTER 8

THE WIZARD CASTS A SPELL:BEWARE THE PREDATORS

ost men are innately good. Most men don't really want to hurt women. In fact, they often have no idea that they do. Men get hurt by women, just as women get hurt by men. Unfortunately, that is part of most relationships. We are all human. However, some men are worse than others in relationships. Some guys have certain tendencies or personalities that are more than frog-like, they are downright predatory. These men should be avoided at all costs, regardless of how wonderful they may seem on the surface, or how handsome they are, or how much money they have.

The wizard, in his extensive wisdom, knew these predatory types existed in his kingdom. In fact, some had dated Princess Kate, and a couple she had even fallen for, like Jonathan who was always on the prowl looking for new girls to hook-up with. When the wizard saw his Kate getting bamboozled by these guys, it made him despise them even more. He knew they were out for their own personal gratification and selfish desires. He'd been around enough to know that it took an awful lot of looking to see past their smooth, seemingly perfect exterior. He also knew that once these guys got their victims under their spell, it was very hard for the girls to break away. And even if the girls did get away, they were left with wounds and scars that may never heal properly.

He saw these guys as kingdom predators, and he wanted to do something about it so that as few girls as possible would be entrapped by their cunning ways. He figured that Princess Kate was probably smart enough to be able to figure out how to find a prince just by having the guys all turned into frogs. But he was worried what would happen when the spell was broken by Kate kissing her Prince Charming, and all the guys were turned back into humans again. He still felt an obligation as kingdom wizard to do all he could to safeguard the other girls in the kingdom. So, after he saw that the frog spell was working so well, he decided to cast a second spell.

The second spell was designed to turn predator-type guys into the animal whose predatory behavior they most resembled. That way, he figured, he could at least protect the kingdom girls because the guys would look like animals such as bears, wolves, vultures and so forth.

Casting such a dramatic spell was hard, but the wizard was more than willing to put in the effort because he cared so much for the girls in the kingdom. He wanted more than anything to protect them from becoming victims to these predator-boys. He was sad as he worked on the predator spell, though, because he knew that even though the guys looked like animals, some girls in the kingdom would still fall for them. With a sigh of resignation, he went ahead with the spell knowing he was doing the best thing for the most people.

As the story goes, as soon as Princess Kate and Daniel kissed, the frog-spell was broken and all the guys in the kingdom turned back into humans. That is, all except the predator-type guys. The Wizard's second spell worked as well as the original frog-spell. Suddenly there were several types of predatory animals walking around the kingdom. Even though these predators were animals, they were for the most part very beautiful and elegant. The wizard then understood why some of the girls in the kingdom would fall for them even though they were animals. In some ways they were even more attractive than the human guys in the kingdom.

A DOSE OF REALITY

Wouldn't it be nice if you could spot predators so easily in real life? Predators prey on the vulnerabilities of girls and women. Don't get involved with a predator thinking that they will change if you just care enough. More than likely, they won't

Many predator type men don't realize they are predators. However, many know full well what they are doing. Almost all of them think they can't help it, blaming their manhood, their fathers, society, or even the girl. They never seem to be able to take full responsibility for their behaviors.

No matter why they act like they do, one thing is constant: predators are out for one thing and that is to get what they want in spite of how it hurts others.

The predator's perspective on the world, on dating, on women, and on themselves is a horrible one. They don't have very much going for them in terms of their own sense of self. They may act confident or cocky, but by now you know better than that. They may be successful at school, on the football field, in business, or with girls, but they are failures when it comes to a healthy feeling about who they are, and how they treat other people, especially women.

Because predators are so dangerous, one thing must be stressed and stressed again:

DO NOT GET MIXED UP WITH A PREDATOR THINKING HE WILL
CHANGE...MOST WON'T. EVEN IF HE DOES CHANGE,
YOU WILL BE HURT LONG BEFORE HE DOES.

THE AGE OLD PLOY: "IF YOU LOVE ME, THEN YOU WILL"

Predators use many different ploys to get what they want from you. If a guy is pressuring you to do something you don't want to do, such as have sex, or to do something that is against your values or beliefs, watch out. Especially if he uses the age-old ploy, "If you love me, then you will...." Run as fast as you can. This is a manipulation to try to get what he wants and nothing more. And it won't be the last time he uses it on you. This is a predator ploy. Any guy who uses this type of ploy to get what he wants is only thinking about himself. It doesn't matter how much he acts like he cares about you, he doesn't really care if doesn't respect your wishes. You should get out as fast as you can, because he will try to get you to do other things that you don't want to do.

HIS SHOWPIECE

If a guy uses you as a showpiece to show off to his friends, be careful! Even if he is the best looking guy in the world, the ultimate catch, you don't want to be his arm candy or his trophy. Eventually, you may realize that you have been used by this guy. It's almost a sure thing.

For instance, Cathy fell for the school hunk. She thought she had really made it when he asked her out. Not long after they began dating, the guy actually began picking out which clothes she would wear to parties. He told her how much weight to lose. He ordered her food on dates, even though it was often not what she wanted to eat. And he manipulated her daily. He had "suggestions" for just about every aspect of her life.

At first, Cathy felt that she was being taken care of and it felt real good. She had never had anybody pay this much attention to her. She was anxious to please him. He was such a catch! But after awhile it got old. She was not happy. He was controlling every aspect of her life. By then, it was hard to break it off because he had such a strangle hold on her. She felt even worse when she found out that he was "messing around" with other girls. He told her that she should be glad that she was his main squeeze, because so many other girls wanted him. He also told her that the others didn't mean anything to him, that she was his true love and that they would always be together. She was so confused that she didn't know what to do. She stayed with him for a long time and when she finally tried to break it off, she was afraid he would hurt her. Finally, breaking up with him was one of the scariest things she ever did. She was never quite the same after that experience. She had less confidence in herself, in her ability to choose good guys, and in her value as a person. This type of guy is showing signs that he is a predator (see the fox, wolf, and boa constrictor descriptions below).

BUT HE SEEMS SOOOOOOOO COOL!

Nothing is cool about physical and mental abuse! Nothing is cool about a teen pregnancy! Nothing is cool about drug and alcohol abuse! Keep all of these things in mind when you are dating. No matter how slick he talks or how sexy he walks - if any of the predators identified sound like your guy - BEWARE! You have such a great life in front of you, don't waste it, ruin it or jeopardize it while you're young.

Young girls that hook up with these types of guys have many misfortunes. Some end up with bulimia, anorexia, depression, insecurity, pregnancy, etc. Any guy or situation that drives you to these behaviors and feelings should be avoided.

There are many types of predatory personalities. Many of them are very similar to animals found in the animal kingdom. That is why the Wizard cast the spell the way he did. The different types of animals out there are described below. Read the descriptions carefully so you can learn by reading about them rather than through actual experience with them. Understand that you may not be able to see these traits clearly at first. Some predators don't fit neatly into one category or another, but if you see any of these characteristics in a guy you are dating, you should be on your guard.

THE MURKY WORLD OF PREDATORS

Some predators are worse than others, but all should be avoided. If you date any of the types described below, it should be only after they are reformed, not in hopes of helping them reform. Do not date a predator type thinking they will change. You can't afford the gamble and the risks are too high. You, your life, and your future depend on avoiding these animals. Those are pretty high stakes. To help you discover if you are involved with a guy that is a predator type, read on...

As you read, be honest with yourself. Don't make excuses for him. It could cost you too much.

THE LION KING

X   He is too busy being impressive to really care about others.

X   He is definitely handsome and regal looking, or acts the part. But this is usually a cover for a fragile self-concept.

X Only people who can do things for him or who can increase his social status deserve his attention.

X At some point, he considered you as someone who could improve his status, otherwise he wouldn't have bothered with you.

X He refuses to put himself out because he thinks others will always come to him, and they usually do, especially women.

X He lets the girl do the work and then takes all the credit or takes first place in line (she works and he benefits).

X He takes care of himself first, then if there is anything left over he will let you have some.

X He dominates. It's his way or no way.

X He uses intimidation to gain control.

X If you don't live up to his expectations of queenly regalness, he will either dump you or keep you and find another woman as well.

THE LAUGHING HYENA

X He loves to play games with your mind.

X He's one of the meanest and strongest predators but his seemingly laughing nature makes it hard to see that. He will even take on a lion if the lion has something that he wants badly enough.

X He is sarcastic, usually at your expense.

X He seems to like you, and then does something to throw you off balance — keeping you wondering all of the time.

X He spends his time testing those around him.

X He pretends to like other girls to see if it can make you jealous.

X He strings you along, and you never know where you stand with him.

X You find yourself frustrated or jealous but afraid to turn away for fear that he will bite you from behind.

X He is constantly saying, "I was just kidding," "Oh, you're just paranoid," or "Can't you take a joke?"

X   He may not be the best looking guy around, but he is hard to resist because he is so tenacious.

X   He is often addicted to drugs, sex or pornography. This is partly because he doesn't think he is addicted, partly because he thinks it is his prerogative, and partly because he thinks that everything is just a joke and so is "addiction."

THE SHARK (ONE OF THE WORST PREDATORS)

X   Everything exists to serve his needs.

X   He is selfish and full of himself.

X   He takes what he wants any way he can get it, even if it means stealing or hurting other people.

X   He manipulates.

X   He can sense weakness or need from great distances

X   He uses charm and his sleek looks as his greatest weapon.

X   He makes you think he is the greatest guy in the world, and is never serious about much of anything.

X   He does whatever he needs to win you over.

X   He rarely pays for you, stating that in these times of equality, the woman should pay her share.

X   He takes advantage of trust and takes people for everything they're worth.

X   He may drain your bank account and max out your credit cards.

X   He generally does not inquire deeply into your life.

X   He is underhanded and sneaky, and has lots of secrets.

X   He feels no empathy or guilt. Everything in the ocean is there just for him.

X   If you stop giving him what he wants, he disappears from your life, but only after he has taken a few chunks out of you emotionally, financially or otherwise.

X   He views life as a "dog-eat-dog-world" and he is one big dog (or shark) that eats many others.

X   He thinks, "If you are strong and smart enough, you can get what you want."

X   He does not like you inquiring about his past. He avoids the subject whenever it comes up.

X   He may have a criminal record, but he says it wasn't his fault. It was always the other guy, or the stupid cop's fault, or the lousy attorney he had.

X   He thinks that loneliness, sadness and joy are all irrelevant. Those are just silly emotions. What matters is what you get from life.

X   He feels nothing. It is hard for you to comprehend that anybody could be that cold so you keep looking for the "good guy" in there somewhere.

X   Sometimes you stay with him because you'd rather be on his side than have him turn against you.

X   And the big one: He's nice to you, but only to get what he wants from you.

THE VULTURE

X   He will circle and circle until he is sure you can be had, then he will hit you when you're down.

X   He looks for your weakness and vulnerability - and uses them to work his way into your life.

X   He likes it when you have low self-esteem because he can control you with his jabs and remarks.

X   He is very patient, waiting for you to give in, at which time he has you right where he wants you.

X   Sometimes you look up and see him circling, you know he is coming after you, but you feel helpless against him so you give in.

✗ He belittles and insults you.

✗ His purpose is to keep you down so he can feel superior.

THE GRIZZLY BEAR

✗ Strong and powerful, he seems like someone you would want to protect you.

✗ From a distance he looks lovable and cuddly.

✗ Once you get close to him the trouble starts.

✗ The closer you get to him, the more unpredictable he becomes. That is what is scary about him: at a distance he seems so fluffy and attractive, but once you get within his range he is all claws and fangs.

✗ He is controlling and has a terrible temper.

✗ He abuses you, sometimes sexually or physically, but always verbally.

✗ The thing he hates most of all is relationship surprises. This brings out the animal in him.

✗ Sometimes he rages over seemingly nothing, just to rage. It makes him feel better, but it is scares you to death. You never know how to act or feel when he does it.

THE CHAMELEON

✗ He is a master manipulator.

✗ He changes with the environment and appears as anything he thinks you want him to be.

✗ He experiences emotion and he usually wants to feel closeness, but he hasn't had his needs met enough in his life, so he feels like he has to trick people to get what he wants.

✗ He shows his true color only after you are emotionally committed.

X He makes friends with your friends, brothers, sisters, or even parents in order to get close to you and to uncover what you want in a male.

X He finds out exactly what you want then says or does just that. He finds out what kind of guy you want, what qualities are important to you, what you find attractive, how you like to be treated and then he does all those things, but only as a ploy to win you over, not as a true change.

X He will become exactly what you want, e.g., changes hair color, hair style, clothes style, musical preferences, religions, everything but his gender (hey, there's an idea) until he has you.

X He calls you incessantly, leaves countless messages on your machine, write notes and letters and tries to work through your friends.

X He is very persistent and has one goal: winning you over.

X He continues to work on you until he wears you down.

X You finally agree to date him because although at first you may not have been attracted to him, after a while he seems that he has most of the things you are looking for in a guy. He just keeps paying attention to you, which doesn't seem altogether bad.

X Once you are entrapped, he will go back to doing what he wants.

X He tends to go after girls that everyone else is after.

X He has a hard time accepting "no" as an answer.

X Rules mean far less to him than what he wants.

X He has difficulty with laws, authority figures, and anything that seems to cramp his style.

X This is the kind of guy about whom women say, "He changed completely after we got married."

THE BULL ELK

X Although not technically a true predator, his behaviors still serve his purposes and not yours, so he is to be avoided like all the other predators.

X He is very showy.

X   He is a smooth talker.

X   It is important to him to have a lot of woman notice him.

X   He prefers to have a harem (multiple women with whom he has a relationship).

X   He likes to play the field and keep all of his women on the line.

X   His life is geared towards collecting women.

X   He will fight viciously with any guy who tries to take one of "his" women.

X   He makes you feel somewhat important because he fights for you so intensely when there is a threat of losing you.

X   He never really listens because he is so caught up in himself.

X   He has similar tendencies as the Lion King, but without the teeth. However, he is willing to fight to get what he wants or to defend what he thinks is his (that means you).

X   He wants only the best, even if someone else has it. He makes this abundantly clear. He makes you think that he sees you as the best. What it really means is that he is the best because he gets all he wants.

X   He is uncommonly shallow, but you would never know it until you get to know him.

THE MONGREL

X   A mongrel is a dirty, flea-bitten, scroungy dog, even though he may not look like it on the outside.

X   Conquest is his goal.

X   The more he gets, the better he feels about himself—for a while.

X   Soon nothing that you have is good enough and he becomes insulting and demeaning.

X He prohibits you from seeing friends.

X He doesn't want you to talk on the phone.

X He may control your money.

X He may ask you to forsake your family, because they don't understand him like you do.

X He doesn't want you to work or have contact with the outside world. He may say that it is because he wants to take care of you , but in reality it is because he's afraid you may get "ideas" about leaving him or that what you have with him is not enough.

X He can be insanely jealous and may decide to hit you or intimidate you to "show you the way it's gonna be."

X He accuses you of looking or wanting other men and flies into rages even if you deny it. This comes from insecurity. He is probably the one doing the looking (at other women, that is).

X He is not picky, he'll date and be with just about anyone.

X He may be addicted to sex, which means he can't really be intimate with anyone.

X He chooses women that are young and immature, because he thinks that they are easier to fool.

X He often becomes abusive, blaming you because you drove him to it.

THE BIRD WITH A BROKEN WING

X He draws you in with a hurt look. He wants you to take care of him.

X He looks for women who love to nurture and make things better.

X He makes you think that if he could only have your sympathy and help, he would be OK.

X He is constantly talking to you about his problem.

X   You find yourself spending many evenings just helping him figure it all out.

X   He calls you almost every day.

X   He often apologizes for taking up so much of your time, which of course leads you to feel even sorrier for him.

X   You look at him as one with "potential" and think you can help him be what he should be.

X   You find he is taking a lot of your time.

X   You feel emotionally drained after you are with him.

X   He can't really get it together because he is still trying to figure himself and everything else out.

X   He can draw very sharp women to him because they want to help.

X   You feel sympathy for him so it is very difficult to impossible to break off any relationship with him.

X   What he really needs is a licensed therapist who can help him sort things out.

THE HORNED TOAD

X   He is always looking for an opportunity to be with a woman sexually.

X   He hangs out at the bar, clubs, dance halls, raves, parties, etc., looking for a woman that may want some sexual activity that night too.

X   He has no problem with one-night stands.

X   You can't trust him. He doesn't expect to be trusted. The only thing he thinks you want is to hook-up.

X   He is always looking for another woman, even when you are with him. He is always on the prowl.

X   Sex is about fulfilling his selfish desires, nothing more, nothing less.

X   If you get into a relationship with this guy chances are very high he won't be faithful.

THE BOA CONSTRICTOR

X   He seems both scary and intriguing at the same time. You want to run but there is something about him that keeps you intrigued.

X   Once he gets you, he draws you into his coils and slowly wraps you up little by little until you are completely wrapped up.

X   At first the wrapping may feel good and comfortable. But once he has you wrapped up he will continue to squeeze you tighter and tighter until you are so trapped that you can't breath or move without his permission.

X   This process is so gradual that you don't even realize that it is happen ing until it is too late.

X   Eventually, he will tell you what to do, what to wear, how you should look, and even how you should feel.

X   Once he has coiled you tightly, he may even begin telling you that he never really loved you, or that you were never really what he wanted, but he will never let you go.

X   If you do manage to get away from him you will have been "crushed" physically and emotionally. You can recover but it will take some work on your part.

KOMODO DRAGON

X   The komodo dragon is the largest lizard on the earth. It eats what ever it wants. But it doesn't get its prey by catching it and immediately consuming it. The komodo often bites the leg or some part of the victim's body and allows the deadly bacteria in his saliva to infect the wound and spread disease throughout the victims body until it dies or becomes too weak to fight. Then the dragon has his dinner.

X   He systematically undermines your confidence with small put downs.

X   In relationships, the komodo dragon-guy will inflict small, seemingly harmless wounds in you. Each wound (usually emotional) is delivered with sarcasm, humor, innuendo, or small insults.

X   He waits until the accumulated wounds have such a weakening effect on you that you think you can't get anything better. In fact, you may become so emotionally wounded that you may not even think you deserve him. When he tells you this you believe him. By this time you are just glad to have him because nobody else would want anything as pathetic and wounded and worthless as he has convinced you that you are.

X   He tells you often that you are lucky to have him and to shut up and mind your own business.

X   He is very strong, and any attempts you make to pull away, especially in your emotionally weakened state, are met with anger and disgust. He makes sure you understand that you are only around because he wants to keep you around and that if you were out on your own you wouldn't last a minute without him.

THE WOLF

X   The wolf runs in packs.

X   You will almost always find him with his friends. His buddies are the most important people in his life. He may spend time with or talk to his guy friends everyday.

X   He spends so much time with his friends, you feel like he is more interested in them than you.

X   He might use his buddies to help him get his girls.

X   He appears confident and self-assured.

X   He will quickly tell you he loves you. He knows that's what you want to hear and he knows it will help him get what he wants.

X   He acts like the "alpha male." He is almost everything stereotypical about guys.

X   Once he has identified his girl "objective," he relentlessly pursues her with out tiring.

X   Once you are in a relationship with him, the animal strength becomes scary.

X   He almost always becomes violent at some point in the relationship. He uses violence when he is worried about losing you.

X   He often drinks or uses drugs and gets mean and ugly when he does.

X   He tells you that you would be nothing without him.

X   You feel that you can't get away because he will always come after you.

THE FOX

X   Have you ever heard the saying: "As sly as a fox." It is a well deserved description. The fox is particularly sly.

X   He is handsome and clever. Almost everybody finds him attractive.

X   He finds ways to get you to notice him, and once you do, he gives you the slip. Naturally your interest is piqued and you begin the chase.

X   As you chase him, he will let you see just enough of him to keep you coming.

X   He seems to be able to talk his way out of almost anything.

X   He lets you know just enough of him that you think you do know him. But usually he has many dark secrets. If you are with him long enough these secrets begin to get revealed little by little. You may not want to believe them because they are so contrary to the other side of him that you have come to know (or think you know).

X   He is one that also tells you early and often that he loves you. He continues to tell you this, usually as a means of keeping you off your guard and away from his hidden self.

X   He is often in or has had legal trouble. If you know about it or find out he seems able to explain it away as "a one time thing," or "a mistake," or "I won't do it again, so you shouldn't worry about it."

X   He makes you feel that all is well, but underneath he is often using you for his own satisfaction.

X   His form of maltreatment is more subtle than using violence. Remember, he is sly. He craftily works your emotions and basic desire to trust to carry on with his dark, hidden life.

X   He controls you with his lies. You may even catch him in his lies, but down deep you want to believe him so you let it go.

X   He is, or has been, involved with other girls. But he convinces you that all the other girls in his life never understood him nor did they mean anything to him. He tells you over and over that you are the only one that really matters.

X   He often defines himself as a victim of abuse, abandonment, society or the system. This is designed to make you feel sorry for him, even though his stories never seem to make complete sense or be completely consistent.

X   He monitors your contact with the outside world because he is afraid you might find out information about him that he doesn't want you to have.

X   He may degrade you and others, but he does it so smoothly that you may not even realize it at the time.

X   He doesn't want you talking to his previous girlfriends or wives, because he thinks they are out to get him and so they will try to convince you that he is manipulative and not good for you.

X   Once you find out about his dark side, you can hardly believe it. It will seem like he is two people. It will take some time for you to come to believe that he is both people and can't be trusted.

These categories describe some of the worst men and most horrible predators. You may have been with a guy that fits into one or even more than one description. If the guy you are with fits most of but not all the points in any one category, that does not mean he isn't that type of guy. Trust the descriptions and your intuition. If he fits most of the points, he is a predator!

The above categories describe very disturbed guys that will be nothing but trouble in a relationship. Avoid them!

INTIMACY AVOIDERS

After the wizard observed all the different predators that his spell created, he was a bit surprised to see a few other types of animal show up as well. He noticed that these other types of animals, while not really predatory in the true sense of the other predators, were still unhealthy for relationships. He decided to call them "Intimacy Avoiders."

They are usually pretty good guys. They don't cause trouble nor are they as abusive as some of the predators. They are guys who want to be in a relationship but don't have the skills to get close enough to another person to create and maintain a fulfilling relationship. Being in a relationship with these types will likely lead to frustration, questioning your judgment, arguments because you want more and dissatisfaction with the relationship.

The following are descriptions of the most common Intimacy Avoiders:

THE STRAY CAT

X   You had to chase him and when you finally got together, he found that the closeness was too much.

X   He is sociable, but doesn't really like parties, dances, etc.

X   He may have a history of being hurt.

X   Just when you think you have shared some very intimate time together, he will do something such as pick a fight or start an argument to create some emotional distance.

X   He avoids the possibility of rejection.

X   He is not very verbal. He only says what he needs to in order to maintain the relationship. This may not be as much as you would like but it may just be barely adequate to be acceptable. You might even think it is "as good as it is going to get" so you stay with him.

X   He dislikes conflict and leaves or stays away if there is conflict.

X   He has difficulty committing to a deeper relationship or marriage, not because he has someone else, but because he is afraid of closeness.

X   He spends hours watching television, fishing, working on projects, surfing the Internet, or some other activity to avoid closeness and dealing with intimate relationships.

X   He has learned to bury his feelings so he doesn't have to deal with them.

THE SPARROW

✗   He is not out to actually harm you or anyone. He thinks his behavior is harmless which makes it even harder for him to make any significant change.

✗   He is a "bird of a feather." In other words, he likes to flock together with his buddies.

✗   He vanishes day after day from responsibilities, and flocks to the boys in the bar, hunting, playing sports, fishing and any other activity that he can do with the guys.

✗   Otherwise he is a good man, a responsible provider and an honorable person.

✗   He doesn't have sexual affairs in the usual sense with other women, but his emotional distance feels like an affair because you feel you are competing against his friends for his attention.

✗   It usually won't matter how much you beg him, he feels a great obligation to be with his male friends. He wouldn't let them down for anything. You feel like you don't come first in his life.

✗   He is continually unavailable physically (because he is gone with his friends). This is by design. It makes him unavailable emotionally.

✗   Often, to him, the male camaraderie is better than the activity itself. It doesn't really matter what he and his buddies do. The important thing is that they are together.

✗   He probably wouldn't participate much in these activities if he had to do it alone.

✗   He wishes you would understand how relaxing and important it is for him to be with other guys.

✗   He thinks it is more work to be with women.

✗   He doesn't understand women. They just don't like to do the same things guys do so what's the use of trying?

✗   His idea of closeness is sex. When you want more (like holding and talking together), he says that you should know how much he cares about you, because he brings home the money. He doesn't understand why you need more, because he doesn't.

X   In reality, he fears intimacy. He doesn't know what to do with it.

THE MOLE

X   He is a loner, insisting on being alone.

X   He disappears into TV, the shop, computer games or programming, reading, or any other solo activity.

X   The only real difference in behavior from that of the Sparrow is that he avoids intimacy by engaging in solo activities.

X   He has never felt comfortable with social activities, either because he thinks he stinks at it or because he has been embarrassed when he expressed his emotions in the past.

X   If there is any conflict at all, he goes away for even longer.

X   He does not like to meet problems head on.

X   He generally runs away from conflict and problems.

X   He is an introvert. At first his introversion might be seen as shyness but it soon becomes clear that it is much more than being shy. It is a defense mechanism to avoid any unwanted interaction with others.

X   He wishes emotions could be downloaded from the Internet, in privacy.

The predators and intimacy avoiders described here are much worse than the frogs discussed in the rest of the book. They are not good in relationships. They cause pain and dissatisfaction in any intimate relationship.

A good example of a relationship with a predator was Cheryl and Greg. Cheryl literally "found" herself in a relationship with Greg that she had no intention of being in. When Greg first asked her out she said, "no." She wasn't very attracted to him. After several attempts asking her out, Cheryl finally agreed to go to lunch. (After all, how committal is a lunch, it's only an hour, right?) Greg was so nice at lunch and presented himself like he was "all together" and had it all. Cheryl decided to go out on one evening date with him, and then a second, a third, and so on.

Greg drove a nice car (only to find out it wasn't his). Greg seemed together business wise, and invested in real estate at auctions (only to find out he used his dad's check book). He traded stocks (only to find out he was involved in an illegal scheme). He wore only the nicest clothes, dropped the right names and seemed too good to be true. (He was.)

After several months in the relationship, Cheryl noticed that Greg was a bit more vocal in her life. He would get upset when she would highlight her hair, because he thought the natural look was much better. He began telling her what to do with career decisions. And he started pushing the sexual intimacy envelope, much further than Cheryl was comfortable with.

Cheryl's family was alarmed. They saw the changes in Cheryl. Instead of being this independent, bubbly person, she was becoming much more dependent on Greg. When Cheryl had her foot operated on, it was Greg that waited for her outside of the recovery room—pushing Cheryl's mom aside.

Cheryl was a smart girl, and she too noticed the changes in her life. She tried to break it off, but Greg kept coming back. This wore Cheryl down, and she agreed to go out with him again. He seemed to have become again what she saw in him at first. They dated for a few more months, only to have Greg start his charades all over again.

The last time Cheryl tried to break up with Greg, he became very insistent over his love for her. He told her they were supposed to be together, and that without him she couldn't be guaranteed a wonderful life. He alone could give it "all" to her.

The following weeks he did things to try to win her back. He left notes on her car window. He called and left love messages on her answering machine. He would wait for her after work to walk and talk with her. He kept pressuring her and telling her how much he cared. She finally agreed to go on one more date with him. He took her for a drive up into the mountains and when he got her isolated he actually proposed marriage to her, and pulled out a ring (a big one that he thought Cheryl couldn't refuse). Cheryl was so mad that she screamed at him to leave her alone. She wanted to jump out of the car and run home but she realized that she was a long way from home and up a mountain in the dark. This made her even more upset. She realized how vulnerable she was. Greg could have done anything he wanted to her. She then got very scared. She insisted that he take her home. Fortunately for Cheryl, Greg did take her home without doing anything to her.

When he dropped her off he told her he loved her. She was too frustrated to respond but jumped out of the car and ran into the house. Cheryl hoped that she was done with Greg but he still tried several times to call her. After a few weeks, he finally left her alone. But he left a definite mark on her. She was afraid of guys for a long time after that. She was always more cautious about where she would go with them. She always made sure that they went places where other people were. It took her several years to really feel that she was rid of him. And when she saw him around town now and then, she would get the most awful, sick feeling in the pit of her stomach.

Later she found out that he had become involved with another girl who wasn't quite as strong as Cheryl. He had gotten the new girl pregnant. They agreed to marry, but on the day before the wedding he told her he didn't love her, never had and never would. She called off the wedding even though she felt deep shame about the whole situation. Greg had played his little game to the ultimate end, and scarred her life.

Cheryl thought she saw him one day way off in the distance. He was looking for his next "adventure." She watched as he slithered away and transformed into The Chameleon.

Like Cheryl experienced with Greg, the problem with these predators is that it is hard to get out of the relationship with them. This may be because women are afraid of them if they should leave. Women might be worried about their physical safety. Because they have been so beaten down emotionally they have very little self-esteem left so they may be worried that they can't make it alone. It might be due to the guy's ability to manipulate women and take advantage of their desire to be in a relationship. Some women see the time spent in a relationship as an investment and find it hard to consider giving up on the investment. These guys sense that and use it against the woman. There might be other reasons it is hard to get out of the relationship, but it is almost always very difficult to get out.

If you find that you are in a relationship with one of these types, for your own sake, get out, no matter how hard it is. Whatever it takes, get out. How, you might ask? The first thing to understand is that you are capable of surviving on your own. If you don't believe this right now go back to chapters 2 and 3 and reread and work on the things talked about there. Work on yourself. Regain your individual strength.

There are resources available through the community to help you get out of threatening relationships. Go to your school counselor or leaders. Contact a safe house or women's shelter. They will know specific resources in your community.

Tell someone what is going on, either your parents, a family member, or close friend. If you are in therapy for any reason, tell your therapist. He or she will also know what to do, who to talk to, and what your options are.

The important thing is that you don't stay in the relationship, no matter how long you have been going together or how much you have invested. Don't allow yourself to be talked into coming back to him. Especially based on promises of "I'll do better," or "I'll change, I'll do anything you want me to," or "I love you. Don't do this to me or us." Those are very common desperate attempts to get you back, and even though it may seem that he is sincere, there is no way he can change that quickly. If he wants to change, let him change without you.

LEST YOU THINK ALL BOYS AND MEN ARE FROGS OR PREDATORS

iz initially didn't consider John serious dating material, because well, he wasn't 6'1" tall with dark hair, as she had always dreamed her prince charming would be. And she was dating someone else when he first asked her out. Even though the current relationship she was in wasn't working out very well, she had a lot invested in it and wanted to keep it going.

John was only 5'11" and had sandy-blonde hair. His body stature was muscular, instead of long and lean like she had dated in the past. But she accepted a date with him even though he wasn't her "dream-guy." She kept going out with him because he was nice, smart and attractive. Besides, she enjoyed herself immensely when she was with him.

She was so impressed with his many good qualities that she thought of lining him up with her best friend. He was too good a catch to let get away, but for someone else, because she always had someone or something else in mind.

However, she found herself continually saying "yes" to dates with him because she enjoyed his company and she could be herself—something she found difficult with the guys that she had been dating. After dating John for a few months, the thought of lining him up with someone else disappeared.

John and Liz would often have long talks about various subjects. Liz always left their dates feeling invigorated about life and her surroundings. John was very respectful of Liz, her time and her dreams. He would help her find solutions to her life's challenges, without taking over.

For the first time, things just seemed to be going right in a relationship. There was no fighting about trivial little things, no wondering where she stood in the relationship, no mind games, no sarcasm in their interaction.

John was truly interested in Liz. He cared about her well-being and they both felt like being better people when they were together. He was great with children, which was something she always wanted in a guy. He was smart academically, again, something Liz always wanted. They had shared interests. They wanted the same things from life. And he was such a gentleman.

When John proposed to Liz on their one year dating anniversary, she said "yes" without hesitation because she realized that, for the first time, her heart and her head were telling her the same thing. She found her prince because she had prepared herself all her life to recognize a good thing when she found it, and because she waited for just the right guy.

CONCLUSION

Remember, remember, remember: you are a valuable person. You deserve the best. Take care of yourself. Get involved only with those who truly encourage and uplift you. If they don't, get them out of your life.

May God bless you in your journey through life and may you always know the frogs from the princes.

APPENDIX

WHEN TO SEEK THERAPY?

There are times in most of our lives when we have difficulties that we need help with. In relationships, the likelihood of having difficulties increases because now we have another person that is creating many situations that have a potential to challenge us and our world. Sometimes we can talk to a friend or family member about our difficulties. Sometimes this helps, sometimes it only makes it worse because we involve someone else in our affairs that have no business being there. Sometimes the best choice by far is professional counseling with a licensed therapist who is trained to handle the particular types of difficulties that we are going through.

You should think seriously about seeking help from a licensed therapist if:

- ♛ You seem to keep choosing the same type of guy, none of whom treats you well.

- ♛ You don't feel worthy of being with a good guy.

- ♛ You are turned off by guys who are nice and who seem to want to treat you well.

- ♛ You always seem to want to "heal" guys who are "wounded." Remember, these guys may put on the wounded act as a predatory technique to draw you in. A licensed therapist is what they need, not a woman who "is the only one in the world who really understands" them.

- ♛ You have ever been in a violent relationship.

- ♛ You have been physically or sexually abused and haven't resolved it.

- ♛ You have a dream/fantasy that someone is going to come along and "take you away from all your misery and troubles," a knight in shining armor on a white horse.

- ♛ The guys you date seem to run, not walk away, complaining that they never know how to act with you.

- ♛ You're afraid of being without a guy.

CHOOSING A THERAPIST

If you find that any of the above situations describe you, it would be advisable for you to seek professional help. But how do you choose a good therapist that will be right for you? Here are a few suggestions when looking for a therapist.

♕ Choose a therapist who comes recommended from someone who saw them for a problem or situation similar to yours, or who knows their work and skills.

♕ Not all therapists are equally good at their profession, and you should seek one out that specializes in dealing with your situation specifically.

♕ Make sure they are licensed and in good standing with the profession al association that oversees them.

♕ Ask them if they have ever been disciplined by their professional organization and for what and what was the result.

♕ Check them out with the Department of Professional Licensing. Information can be found in the state department section of your local phone book to see if any complaints have been filed or actions taken against them.

♕ If all things check out, you will probably be fine getting therapy with that therapist. If after one or two sessions you don't feel comfortable, it would be good for you to express that to the therapist. Give them a chance to understand that things are not going well for you and make changes. If he or she doesn't make changes, then you should change therapists.

Keep in mind, it is your responsibility to work in therapy. The therapist is not supposed to tell you what your problems are, you should be able to come in and set the agenda for therapy. Good therapists will help you work through the issues that you bring to therapy, not provide you with the issues. Try to do what he or she instructs. See the following section if you are doing what your therapist suggests and nothing seems to be changing in your relationship.

CHANGING THERAPISTS

If your therapist just doesn't seem to be meeting your needs, you have the right to choose another therapist. The following questions can help you to decide whether or not to change therapists.

♛ Do I feel comfortable enough to talk about sensitive issues with my therapist?

♛ Does he or she let me share my values, yet challenging me to change the behaviors which prevent me from being happy or healthy?

♛ Am I wanting to change therapists because he or she seems to always ask about the hard issues? If so, this is not a very good reason to change therapists. It means that the therapist is tuned into you and is trying to help. If it is too intense for you, tell your therapist and let them adjust the pace of therapy so it is more comfortable to you. But remember, therapy is not necessarily comfortable. The process of change is often difficult as you face yourself and your issues.

♛ Never change therapists without letting him or her know why so he or she can get feedback on how he or she can improve his or her work. If you have talked to him or her, and nothing changes, feel free to go elsewhere. You are in charge of your treatment.

It is important to know that your therapist should not see you socially, sexually or in a business relationship. A therapist that suggests having a relationship with you outside of therapy (wants to date you, have sex with you, wants to do some other business dealings with you, or does anything else similar) is acting inappropriately and in many cases, illegally. You should let him or her know that it is unacceptable and that he or she is breaking the law. You should consider reporting him or her to the Department of Professional Licensing. You should also look for a new therapist.

ABOUT THE AUTHORS

Klayne I. Rasmussen, Ph.D., is a licensed Marriage and Family Therapist. He has been working in the therapy field since 1992 and has been licensed in Utah since 1997. He received his Ph.D. in Marriage and Family Therapy from Brigham Young University, his Master's degree in Marriage and Family Therapy from Loma Linda University in California, and his Bachelor's of Science degree in Psychology from Brigham Young University. Throughout his career, his emphasis has always been working with relationships, and helping people prepare to have the most fulfilling, healthy relationships possible.

Kip S. Rasmussen, Ph.D., earned his Masters degree in Family Studies from Texas Tech University and graduated from Brigham Young University with his Ph.D. in Marriage and Family Therapy in 1994. Current areas of specialization include parent-child interaction and recovery from eating disorders. He works extensively with teenage girls as they make their journey along the path of self-discovery. He is married with three children and firmly believes that every girl deserves someone who treats her like royalty.

Verena B. Rasmussen is married to Klayne Rasmussen. They have five wonderful boys. She received her Bachelor's of Science degree from the University of Utah in Marketing. She recently concluded a 12-year journey with Salt Lake's Olympic effort. She was the Director of International Client Services for the Salt Lake Olympic Committee until April 2002, when the Games concluded. With only boys, but a good memory of what the dating process was like for her, her hope is that the concepts in the FrogBuster will help many girls in their quest to find their Prince Charming.

Th€ FrogBuster Quick Order Form

FAX this form to (801) 544-2518
PHONE orders to (801) 544-2470
MAIL this form to:

INTRALIFE SYSTEMS PUBLISHING, P.O. BOX 1555
LAYTON, UTAH 84041-6555 USA.

Please send me ___ copies of **The FrogBuster**

@ $16.95 each $_____

Utah residents add 6.5% for sales tax : $_____

Add $3.00 S/H for the first copy

and $1.00 for each additional copy ordered: $_____

TOTAL ENCLOSED: $_____

SHIP ORDER TO:

Name: _____

Address: _____

City: _____ State: _____ Zip: _____

Daytime telephone: _____

Email: _____

PAYMENT:

☐ Check   ☐ Visa   ☐ MasterCard   ☐ AMEX
Card Number: _____

Name on Card: _____

Exp. Date: _____ / _____

Signature: _____

Ṭʜᴇ FʀᴏɢBᴜsᴛᴇʀ Qᴜɪᴄᴋ Oʀᴅᴇʀ Fᴏʀᴍ

FAX this form to (801) 544-2518
PHONE orders to (801) 544-2470
MAIL this form to:

INTRALIFE SYSTEMS PUBLISHING, P.O. BOX 1555
LAYTON, UTAH 84041-6555 USA.

Please send me ___ copies of **The FrogBuster**

@ $16.95 each $_____

Utah residents add 6.5% for sales tax : $_____

Add $3.00 S/H for the first copy

and $1.00 for each additional copy ordered: $_____

TOTAL ENCLOSED: **$**_____

....

SHIP ORDER TO:

Name: _____

Address: _____

City: _____State: _____ Zip: _____

Daytime telephone: _____

Email: _____

PAYMENT:

☐ Check   ☐ Visa   ☐ MasterCard   ☐ AMEX
Card Number: _____

Name on Card: _____

Exp. Date: _____/_____

Signature: _____

Tꜧᴇ FʀᴏɢBᴜsᴛᴇʀ Qᴜɪᴄᴋ Oʀᴅᴇʀ Fᴏʀᴍ

FAX this form to (801) 544-2518
PHONE orders to (801) 544-2470
MAIL this form to:

INTRALIFE SYSTEMS PUBLISHING, P.O. BOX 1555
LAYTON, UTAH 84041-6555 USA.

Please send me ___ copies of **Tꜧᴇ FʀᴏɢBᴜsᴛᴇʀ**

@ $16.95 each $_____

Utah residents add 6.5% for sales tax : $_____

Add $3.00 S/H for the first copy

and $1.00 for each additional copy ordered: $_____

TOTAL ENCLOSED: $_____

....

SHIP ORDER TO:

Name: _____

Address: _____

City: _____State: _____ Zip: _____

Daytime telephone: _____

Email: _____

PAYMENT:

☐Check   ☐Visa   ☐ MasterCard   ☐ AMEX

Card Number: _____

Name on Card: _____

Exp. Date: _____ / _____

Signature: _____

IntraLife Systems Publishing
P.O. Box 1555 Layton, Utah 84041-6555 USA